THE
DYNAMICS
OF
ACTING

NATIONAL TEXTBOOK COMPANY • Lincolnwood, Illinois U.S.A.

THE
DYNAMICS
OF
ACTING

JOAN SNYDER

MICHAEL F. DRUMSTA

CREDITS

From NEVER A GREATER NEED by Walter Benton. Copyright 1948 by Alfred A. Knopf, Inc. and renewed 1976 by Walter Benton. Reprinted by permission of Alfred A. Knopf, Inc.

From THE PROPHET by Kahil Gibran. Reprinted by permission of Alfred A. Knopf, Inc. Copyright 1923 by Kahil Gibran, renewed 1951 by Administrators C.T.A. to Kahil Gibran Estate and Mary G. Gibran.

From THE THREE SISTERS by Anton Chekhov; translated from the Russian by Stark Young. Reprinted by permission.

A CONEY ISLAND OF THE MIND by Lawrence Ferlinghetti. Copyright © 1958 by New Directions Corporation. Reprinted by permission of New Directions.

From ARMS AND THE MAN by George Bernard Shaw. Hollywood: Samuel French, Inc.

From ACTING THE FIRST SIX LESSONS by Richard Bolselavsky (New York: Theatre Arts Books, 1949) p. 55.

Joan Snyder, a former high school and university dramatic arts teacher, is currently the Artistic Director of Meadows Playhouse, Las Vegas, Nevada. Michael P. Drumsta is a veteran speech and theatre teacher who now heads his own creative group serving publishers and other organizations in the fields of education and communication. Working with him on this edition of *The Dynamics of Acting* were William F. Sprick, writer; Richard Katschke, editor; Mark Krastof, photographer; and, Gregory Newlin, creative associate.

We wish to thank the theatre directors and their students at the following schools for their cooperation in providing photographic subjects for this edition: Niles West High School, Skokie, Illinois; Evanston Township High School, Evanston, Illinois; The Latin School, Chicago, Illinois; Thornwood High School, Dolton, Illinois; and, The Free Street Theatre, Chicago, Illinois.

1986 Printing

OVERTURE

From almost the beginning of time, human beings have used drama as a basic tool for understanding. When they discovered drama, they found they were able to teach, to understand, to love, to explore, through the experience of others. They found they could discover the heights and depths of emotions and relate them through study and characterization.

As drama's importance progressed over the centuries, so did its values as an understanding of the human condition. Not only were people able to search for the truth in their consideration of others, they certainly were able to understand the self in a far more dimensional vein. To accept the essence of drama is to understand the essence of self; mind, body, and spirit.

Even today, as we consider teaching theatre arts as both a vocation or an avocation, the importance of the self and its understanding of the human condition is ever more important. As students and teachers, we have a great advantage to be able to share the experiences that theatre and drama afford. In few educational situations can the barrier of age and communication be broken—certainly drama provides an exceptional opportunity to break these barriers.

Theatre is a collaborative art. Without any of its levels of creative expertise, a production could not be mounted. What an exciting experience is this edition of *The Dynamics of Acting*. What better way to approach our work than in the format we know best—through scenes and acts, and to be able to achieve our goals through motivational rehearsals.

Robert Johnson
Director of Theatre Program
Niles West High School
Skokie, Illinois

PROGRAM

ACT II

ACT III

EPILOGUE

PROLOGUE

This edition of *The Dynamics of Acting* is an effective program designed for the beginning actor who wants to learn the basic art of the theatre. The novice is lead from scene to scene, first learning the rudiments of acting and then practicing activities designed for the further reinforcement of skills. With the bold new approach for acquiring a time-honored skill, *The Dynamics of Acting* allows the student to experience by actively participating in the learning process.

The building-block approach is used throughout the text in order to take the student step-by-step from the basics of acting to the more complex and difficult techniques used by professional actors. The "Rehearsal Time" activities provide practical exercises to supplement and further reinforce techniques and skills discussed in the text. In this way, the beginning actor will gain self-confidence and also an appreciation for one of the most demanding of the fine arts. Whether the novice becomes a Bernhardt or an Olivier, or simply a theatre consumer, this book is the first important step to an understanding and appreciation of what is involved in acting.

The tone of this text has been kept fresh and informal so that the reading remains practical and interesting. The extensive use of photographs and graphics add to the excitement and immediacy of the acting art and motivate creativity within the performer.

A tri-level structure has been used to give the book the flavor of an actual play in three acts. Within each of the acts, the overall structure is divided into scenes, again following the basic pattern of an actual play. This structure allows for a practical and flexible learning experience in the school situation.

At the end of each scene, there is a section consisting of opportunities for application called "Rehearsal Time." These activities are meant to be used as stepping stones for experimentation and to supply a basis from which the instructor, the director, or even the actor can germinate new exercises of his or her own. The introduction to each scene reviews previous material and previews what is to come. At the end of each scene, the "Curtain" is drawn, summarizing the material presented.

Throughout, the step-by-step approach is continued, so that what is to be learned builds upon what has already been mastered. Because of this basic approach to the learning process, this book can easily be used by any educational theatre group, including community theatre or anyone interested in learning the fundamentals of acting.

Included in the text is information every theatre enthusiast would find invaluable in the further study of the art. An extensive bibliography of additional reading material appears in the Epilogue for additional research and reference. A glossary of theatrical terms including definitions of everyday theatre usage has been added. "The Other Side of the Curtain" describes the duties and responsibilities of the technical crews behind the scenes. Each of the different backstage roles is discussed, providing a brief description of how it affects the entire play production.

Along with these added features, the actual text goes beyond acting on an amateur level, supplying information on professional theatre, theatre on the college level and community theatre. Act Three Scene Three provides students with information on historical theatre periods, as well as the different styles of acting. This provides the actor with a firm historical foundation in the art of acting.

Acting is one of the most exciting and rewarding careers to which a person could aspire, but not everyone will choose to be a professional actor or actress. This edition of *The Dynamics of Acting* also relates to these people, giving them a chance to see what acting is all about by allowing them to experience the thrill of being on stage themselves. This is not meant to be just a training manual for aspiring actors, but a beginning experience and appreciation of the theatre.

Acting is exciting for both the professional and the amateur. With time and patience, a proficiency can be obtained in the basics of acting. This book is aimed at this specific objective. Anyone can enjoy the satisfaction of learning to direct energy into giving a performance for the enjoyment of others. This book will help direct that energy and supply the basics for teaching others to feel, to understand, to imagine. With work, time, and patience, the joy of performing can be achieved by anyone. This text will add to the pleasure of learning the techniques necessary for achieving these goals.

Scene One

BASIC BEGINNINGS

Acting involves every part of the performer. The mind, body, voice, and even one's will play important parts in creating a character that lives within the framework of a play. Once it is understood that an actor uses all of the physical and mental resources available, the structure of acting can be better appreciated. Creativity begins with the knowledge and application of the body. It also involves discipline of the mind and use of the will to control and generate the performance. Putting all of these powers together is the first step in creating, which is the first step toward acting and performing.

Theatrical Physique

Everyone is an individual. Thus, everyone is distinct and different from the next person. Each actor's uniqueness must become a focal point of awareness. Generally, older people have an advantage over younger people because they have more years of self-awareness.

Self-awareness

Opening up to a group of people both physically and mentally is a frightening thought. It may take some time to overcome self-consciousness. It is a condition that every actor experiences to some degree. Uneasiness in front of people, however, can be used to an advantage. This nervous energy can be channeled into character energy, which helps to give more life on stage. Through determination and repetition of the proper exercises, the process of developing into an actor will be achieved.

There are many forces working against an actor's desire for self-awareness. There is always the fear of the unknown. Laziness, at times, can get in the way of an actor's study of self-awareness. However, once the effort and energy is expended to begin this study, the knowledge can be used toward the creation of characters on stage. A character is based on an actor's own experiences, and this knowledge of self enhances stage pres-

Physical and awareness exercises play a vital role in the development of an actor.

ence through power and believability. It heightens the truthfulness and honesty of the portrayal.

It is important to remember that acting is a demanding art. The performer must be physically fit in order to develop correct posture, make fluid gestures and movements, cultivate flawless articulation, and be able to project the script on stage. Proper diet, adequate rest and exercise, as well as periodic check-ups are advised.

Relaxation

Since acting is such a rigorous endeavor that tends to create additional anxiety and tension, one of the problems most actors face is the need for relaxation. Whether it be in class, in rehearsal, in actual stage performance, or off the stage, relaxation is crucial to all performers. Relaxation is not a state of mental and physical inactivity; but rather a positive and active state. It enables actors to express themselves while still controlling the other factors working against clear character portrayal. Thus, relaxation is necessary to achieve the objectives of a performer.

Anything that diverts attention from or interferes with an actor's concentration on character tends to destroy relaxation. A beginning actor usually does not respond easily to the command, "Just relax!" The key to relaxation first involves coming to grips with both the physical and mental aspects of the body. Secondly, confidence must be achieved

while sensitively and clearly projecting emotion and action to an audience. This positive state means that some tension is released while responses to stimulus are still being made that will enhance the portrayal. In other words, when relaxed, the actor should be waiting calmly and alertly for actions or thoughts to take place.

To attain relaxation or any kind of physical or mental control on stage, concentration must be the first objective. There is a very close correlation between the mind and the body. The performer must be able to control the body at all times on stage through the use of the mind. Concentration begins with an understanding of the body and the reasons for its behavior. The first step toward becoming a proficient actor is becoming aware of and being able to use the body efficiently.

REHEARSAL TIME

A large group can participate in each of the following activities at the same time. You will be required to remember these feelings later. After each exercise, record your impressions in a theatrical notebook. List the new information or experiences you gained during your workout.

Catalogue—to remember specific feelings or information encountered during an exercise; the ability to repeat the feeling or information in the future for use on stage or for discussion.

Take space—to find an area in which you can move freely without constrictions, usually an arm's length from anyone or anything else.

Activities

1. Take space on the floor, lying flat on your back. Begin to concentrate on the tips of your toes. Concentrate on totally relaxing every toe. Then concentrate on relaxing your entire foot. Continue to concentrate on relaxing your ankles, then your calves, and so on up the body until every part of your body is in a total state of relaxation. Make sure you are aware of the feeling of your body as it moves from a state of tautness and tension to relaxation. Try to catalogue this feeling of relaxation in your notebook for future reference.

2. After you are totally relaxed,

begin adding tension to every muscle in your body, again working up from the toes. Make sure you are aware of the feeling of your body as your muscles tighten. Catalogue in your notebook this feeling of tautness for future reference.

3. Now that you have slowly relaxed and tightened your muscles, you are ready for the next phase. One person in the group should separate from the others and serve as a monitor. On three-second intervals for thirty seconds, the monitor should clap hands to serve as a signal. Upon this signal, the rest of the group should tighten and relax all of the muscles in their bodies. After thirty seconds, change monitor and repeat the exercise for another thirty seconds. Change monitors several more times to achieve the feel of tightening and relaxing your body. It is important in each exercise for you to remember the feelings you experience.

4. Remain on the floor. Continue to rotate monitors. Extend both of your legs and arms out from your sides, still keeping them on the floor. Imagine someone pulling first your left and then your right leg. React to this feeling. Then, in the same way, imagine someone pulling your left and right arm. Again, let your body react to this feeling. Continue by imagining someone pulling you by the top of your head. React. Repeat the exercise again with the monitor clapping on three-second intervals. Continue repeating this exercise for a three-minute period. In your notebook, catalogue these feelings of being stretched for future use.

5. The monitor should return to the group. Now, imagine you are trying to make yourself as small and compact as possible. Compress your body to the greatest extent that you can. Pull your legs under your chin, double up, and squeeze. Relax. Again compress yourself and squeeze. Remember how it feels to be very small and compact.

6. After you have completed all of these exercises, begin to discuss your impressions of your feelings. How did it feel to be so compact and so stretched out? How did it feel to be very relaxed and very tense? When acting, when would you be in a very relaxed position? When would you be very tense? When would you want to be very compact, and when would you need to stretch to your greatest extent?

7. Make notes in your theatrical notebook of the situations where each of these physical feelings could be used. Describe how you should feel about your body in each situation. Also, record how your body response and muscle control is progressing as you experience new feelings and review old feelings you may have forgotten your body knew.

Theatrical Area

The combination of actors and audience is called a *stage,* and the relationship between the two is the total theatrical experience. In order to begin understanding this experience, the beginning actor must become familiar with some terms relative to moving on stage. The most important thing to remember is that a stage is any area in which actors create experiences for an audience.

The first step in understanding the conventional stage is to become familiar with its different areas. Most stages are arranged with the audience on one side of the actors and a wall or some kind of backdrop on the other. The area closest to the audience is commonly identified in the theatre as *downstage.* The area closest to the back wall or farthest from the audience is referred to as *upstage.*

The dynamics of space appear different to the audience than to the actor. Perspective is relative to the position of the actor and the audience.

Downstage Left	Downstage Center	Downstage Right
Center Left	Center	Center Right
Upstage Left	Upstage Center	Upstage Right

All stage directions are given in relation to the actor's right or left when facing the audience.

Basic Body Positions

Besides the different areas of the stage, the actor should also become familiar with the basic body positions on the stage. While the director may have many variations on the terms and possibly some additional positions, these are the five basic body positions relative to facing the audience.

1. *Full front* is the position in which an actor faces the audience.

2. *Full back* is the position in which an actor stands with his or her back to the audience.

3. *One-quarter position* is a quarter-turn stance away from the audience.

4. *Profile or one-half turn* is the position taken when an actor faces either right or left so that the audience sees the actor's profile.

5. *Three-quarters* is a position in which the actor turns nearly half back, so that less than one side of the head and a shoulder are toward the audience.

For each of the following activities, divide into learning groups with a minimum of three and a maximum of five. These exercises are designed to help you become familiar with the different stage areas and body positions. You will need to become so familiar with the different positions that you could repeat them in your sleep. These positions are fundamental to acting. As an actor, you will be required to know them the rest of your acting life. Make sure you use your theatrical notebook for a written record of this new information.

Dominant—in a stronger position or in a position of prominence; usually the actor that the audience can see the clearest.

Subordinate—in a lesser or weaker position to another actor on stage.

Activities

1. Define a stage area and indicate where the audience and the backstage will be. Move through each of the following areas starting at centerstage. Name each area as you go from one to the next.

- a. Upstage right
- b. Downstage center
- c. Downstage right
- d. Upstage center
- e. Downstage left
- f. Centerstage right
- g. Upstage left
- h. Centerstage left

Repeat this exercise for each person in the group.

2. Now that you have defined the stage areas, again move about the stage adding different body positions.

- a. Centerstage right—Full front
- b. Downstage right—One-half turn left
- c. Centerstage—Full back
- d. Upstage left—Three-quarters right
- e. Downstage left—Full front
- f. Upstage center—One-quarter left
- g. Downstage center—Profile right

Repeat the exercise for each person in the group.

3. Once each person feels comfortable with the different body positions, two of the actors should move on stage while the rest of the group serves as the audience. The actors will move to the different areas of the stage as listed, and the audience members will observe the actors in each set of positions. Each member of the audience will then identify which of the actors on stage seems to be in the dominant and subordinate positions. In this analysis, the audience members should be observing the actors only as bodies on a stage. They should *not* take into account the physical characteristics of each actor, such as height, weight, or sex. The audience should only

be comparing the body positions and the stage areas for strength.

    a. One actor centerstage—One actor upstage right
    b. One actor downstage right—One actor downstage center
    c. One actor downstage left—One actor centerstage
    d. One actor upstage center—One actor downstage center

These body positions should be compared with both actors centerstage.

    e. One actor one-quarter right—One actor one-quarter left toward each other
    f. One actor full front—One actor three-quarters left
    g. Both actors profile facing each other
    h. Both actors profile facing away from each other
    i. One actor three-quarters right—one actor three-quarters left toward each other

Continue repeating this exercise, substituting audience members as actors, until everyone has had a chance on stage.

4. When these exercises are completed, discuss as a group the outcomes of your comparisons. Were certain areas of the stage stronger than others? Were certain body positions stronger than others? Why are these areas or positions stronger, and what does this mean to the actor who is using them?

5. From your memory, draw in your notebook the stage with its areas. Label the audience and the backstage. Label right and left stage. Make a list of each of the body positions, arranging them from strongest to weakest. Make a list of each of the different stage areas, arranging them from strongest to weakest.

Theatrical Movement

There are certain conventions that are commonly used on the stage in regard to movement. These rules are by no means unbendable or unbreakable in the correct situations. The actor must learn when to use the rules to his or her advantage. With insight into and practice of the techniques of acting, these rules become a great help in movement.

Stage movement means a change of position or location on stage. Movement on stage should be motivated or have a reason for happening. There should be no movement on stage without purpose. There are occasions when the director may call for a particular movement to set a specific mood. The motivation for movement needs to be understood by the actor for a clear characterization.

Movement can relax the body so the actor can flow and move around the stage naturally. Body tension, depending on the level and intensity, can obstruct the natural movement of the arms, head, face, and legs.

Basic Principles

When moving on stage, the following basic principles should be kept in mind:

1. Always move in character, or as the character would move.
2. Movement on stage is usually performed in a straight line. (Movement in curved lines is also acceptable in the right circumstances, but is less common.)
3. Movement is usually not made while another character is speaking on stage.
4. When a group enters, the actor who is speaking is usually ahead of the others.
5. All movements should have motivation. Any superfluous movement on stage tends to detract, rather than add, to a characterization. Every movement must count when on stage.
6. Movement should not be overdone without reason.
7. Unless the situation calls for hidden movement, all actors should be seen by the audience when moving.

Even though movement on stage is planned, the actor must constantly strive for a natural look on stage.

REHEARSAL TIME

The following activities are to be done in a large group. Each member of the group will have a chance to perform in each of the exercises. For these activities, it is important to try and use the ideas of movement and space that have been presented. You will need a stage area that is large enough for one to five actors. Keep notes in your theatrical notebook on specific movements that seem particularly effective.

Activities

1. One member of the group should select an emotion (hate, love, anger, fear, peace, happiness, thoughtfulness, worry, nervousness, excitement) and try to portray it through body movement. This can include a walk, the way the actor stands or posture, hand and trunk movements. You should try to incorporate as many meaningful movements as possible. The rest of the group will identify and discuss what emotion is being portrayed. They should focus on what specific movements demonstrated the emotion best.

2. Repeat the exercise using from one to five actors portraying the same emotion at the same time. The audience should be keeping notes on the differences of strength between the actors.

What types of movements tend to make a particular portrayal stronger in the audience's minds? Repeat this activity several times, rotating groups until everyone has been on stage at least once.

3. One actor should stand center-stage with three other actors standing perfectly still behind the speaker. The speaker should recite the "Mary Had a Little Lamb" verse. The speaker should then repeat the recitation while one of the actors moves slowly off stage. This performer should return to the stage. Repeat the activity again, with two performers moving off stage in different directions during the recitation. Repeat a final time, with all three actors moving. Discuss what happened to the impact of the speaker as the others began to move. Why does this happen? What can actors do to prevent this situation? How can actors use this to their advantage?

4. In your theatrical notes, analyze each of the exercises and record what you think might be valuable about various movements. Compare and discuss your notes with other group members. Then revise your record to include some of the group findings that you might not have included originally. Remember to keep notes in your notebook on anything that you may see, either in or out of rehearsal, that might add to your physical awareness of yourself.

CURTAIN

Acquiring knowledge of the body is the first crucial step a potential actor takes. The performer needs to know what makes muscles relax and tighten and how to control it. Body control and discipline are necessary to communicate effectively to the audience. The potential actor's awareness of the role concentration plays in development is also important for theatrical growth.

Some of the exercises in this and the following chapters should prove most helpful if performed more than once or twice. They can be used as warm-ups before rehearsals and as simple muscle awareness exercises at any time. They will help develop the freedom and believability needed for good character portrayal.

The physical fact of being on stage necessitates clear knowledge of the acting areas. Understanding stage terminology is also important to developing a knowledge of stage areas, body positions, and movement. This understanding will lead to a proper orientation of the actor to the audience, to the other performers, as well as to one's own body. The result will be constructive interaction and communication between actor and audience.

Scene Two

BEYOND BASICS

The actor's work truly begins when he or she is placed in a scene as a character. Exploring the environment, the actor must use mental and physical resources. The term *resource* indicates something that is useful and can be called upon when needed. The actor's resources come from remembering past attitudes and actions. These prior experiences can be used to communicate a character to an audience. An actor's resources can originate in senses, feelings, and observations; or, they can originate in the mind or the imagination.

Senses, Feelings, and Observations

Senses and feelings are useful resources when the actor cannot communicate or interpret a character to the audience through words. This is called *nonverbal communication.* There are many levels of nonverbal communication used in the theatre. For example, feelings can be communicated through the eyes and eyebrows, facial expression, hands, and even by silence. All body movement on stage should be pertinent to the particular character and situation being portrayed. In other words, body motion can be meaningless or in some situations wrong, if not used in the correct context of the play. Therefore, every movement should be important and *in character.* This is making the movement a part of and right for the character.

Meaning Through Gesture

Most people do more communicating through their body movement than through their voice. Further, body movement, or nonverbal communication, reveals the inner senses or feelings of most people. For example, at times a person's facial expression might contradict the words being spoken. This means that what is being said is not totally truthful.

In our society, a number of specific meanings are attached to certain gestures or body movements. For instance, a clenched fist and holding one's nose have specific meanings to each of us. Such meanings are attached to behavior patterns we learn from our culture. Performers must be able to recognize and effectively utilize these behavioral aspects of our society. An actor is called upon to portray many different roles in many different situations, yet each character must be individualized in terms of behavior. In addition, each character must be conventional in terms of behavior within society.

The external behavior one projects must not be revealed solely from the outside of the character. Every action, gesture, and signal should have an internal significance. Sniffing the air may give the audience the idea of an odor in the air. This does not, however, reveal the person's feelings about the odor or inner reactions to it.

Finally, the actor must be able to control personal nonverbal tendencies that may not fit a particular character. When personal gestures or body movements do not fit into the make-up of a particular character, they should be curbed even if they are very natural to the actor. The actor's own personal habits are not always fitting or appropriate to a particular character, and only those that are applicable should be used.

Observation and Empathy

Observing is being aware of what is going on in life. People, places, objects, and situations all add to an actor's depth of awareness. When watching people, the actor should constantly be taking mental notes on physical habits and body movements. These mental notes may become the basis for a character in the future. They then can be triggered when needed to create a character's physical movements within the struc-

An actor's senses, feelings, and observations can be primed and expanded through discussion with other actors.

ture of a play. Eventually, these mental notes will become so natural, they become part of the actor, as well as part of the character.

Once these responses are ingrained in the actor, a relationship can begin to form between actor and audience. This relationship is commonly known as empathy. *Empathy* means the flowing of emotion from the actor to the audience and its return. It is an emotional identification between the actor and audience. The audience feels as the actor portraying a character feels. For example, when one person yawns, it is the empathic response for other people to yawn. Or, when a friend loses someone dear, the empathic response is to feel some of the friend's pain.

Successful powers of observation must incorporate empathy with intellectual watchfulness. This means the actor must develop a sensitivity to the senses; sight, touch, smell, hearing, and taste. Recognizing and remembering one's senses during daily activities is very important. To correctly observe, one must be able to perceive and catalogue senses. Thus, senses, feelings, and observations combine to form a chain that implement character creation. An actor must use the powers of observation for the following purposes:

1. to learn human characteristics in walking, gesturing, talking, and sitting, that may be reproduced on stage,
2. to stimulate creative imagination, and
3. to incorporate qualities learned from watching animals. The gracefulness of a cat is an example of an animal characteristic.

REHEARSAL TIME

group should be encouraged to express their ideas to the group as a whole.

Activities

1. Using each of the senses (seeing, hearing, touching, smelling, and tasting), briefly and accurately describe one of the following verbally:

a. campfire smoke
b. a ripe apple
c. silk
d. beach sand
e. salt water
f. ammonia
g. thick, curly hair
h. a shiver
i. an electric mixer
j. a small baby
k. a wool sweater
l. hot tea
m. a feather
n. a smoldering fire
o. air

For each of the following activities, a large group can participate at the same time. These exercises are designed to make you more aware of your senses, feelings, and powers of observation. They can either be performed in a discussion group with everyone participating in turn, or they can be done in smaller groups first. If the latter method is used, the findings of the smaller groups can then be presented and discussed in a large group session. In either case, all of the separate members of the

2. Name the senses you would use in the list of rooms and buildings that follows. How would each room affect you emotionally? Why?

a. toy shop
b. kitchen
c. attic
d. zoo
e. garbage dump
f. produce store
g. park after a rainfall

GEORGIA PEACHES

h. playground
i. movie theatre
j. funeral home
k. doctor's office

3. Relate, step-by-step, to the group the routine you went through *exactly* this morning between the time you woke up and the time you left the house. How good is your memory of these events? What does this say about your powers of observation?

4. During your everyday activities make a conscious effort to observe people and their habits, gestures, and speech patterns. Keep a record in your theatrical notebook of the things you observed. Try to begin cataloging in your mind, as well as on paper, other people's actions and movement patterns. Practice some of these patterns yourself in your spare time.

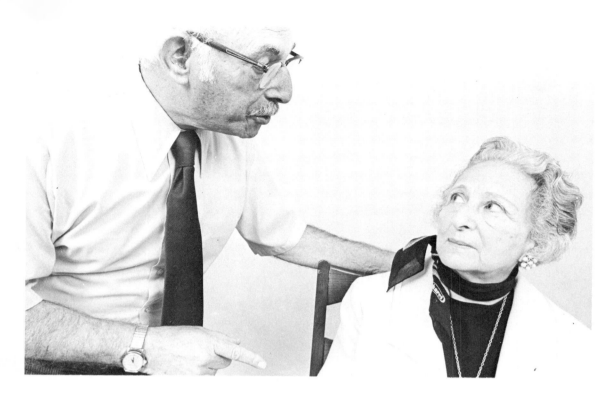

Experiences

The most obvious resources for an actor, and the easiest to grasp, are past and present experiences. The most uncomplicated application of experiences is through oral communication with people. When experiences are related to others, they tend to be related on both a verbal and nonverbal level.

Again, empathy becomes important in the communication of experiences. It is healthy for an actor to recount experiences in front of a group. It heightens the awareness of empathy and gives the performer a chance to communicate vividly to others. If the audience empathizes and becomes involved, the actor then experiences an important part of

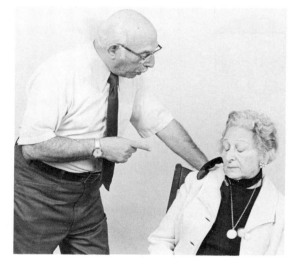

The more mature actor has a wider range of experiences to draw upon to enrich a character.

true acting. When there is active empathy between actor and audience, there is a basis for a good performance.

Past Experiences

The actor uses experience in still other ways. In the course of studying a script or the text of a play, an actor may find situations that are similar to experiences from the past. By drawing on this resource, the actor can add more life and believability to a character portrayal. As a starting point, experiences can be very beneficial to an actor's character building. When the character is based on truth and is believable, the audience can become more involved and empathic.

This exercise should be performed in a large group positioned in a circle.

Activity

1. Every member of the group will be required to stand and relate to the group an experience of emotional impact. While the speaker is relating, the rest of the group should be listening and observing empathic qualities in the story.

After the story has been related, several members of the group should give *constructive criticism* of the performance. This is to point out the strong and weak points of the performance in relation to its empathetic impact. Did the storyteller make you feel what he or she was remembering? How could this feeling have been better related? What were the strong points in the story? How did you feel when the story was over? Why did you feel this way? Is this what you think the storyteller would have wanted you to feel?

Each member of the group should have a chance to tell an experience and have the group comment as a whole. Remember, it is important that the criticism should be constructive in order for the performer and the audience to benefit from it.

Imagination and Pantomime

Visualizing a character through observations and through the senses is a vital, fundamental task of the actor. Perhaps an even more difficult task is to use imagination in acting. When observations and senses cannot completely "fillout" a character, imagination becomes very important.

Imagination

Imagination is the art of forming mental images of what is not actually present. These mental images are created as new ideas or as a combination of past experiences and new ideas. Imagination is based on an actor's own life and past experiences.

Some people have vivid imaginations. They are able to dream up a great variety of images in their own minds either by daydreaming or by extending present situations. For others, highly active imagination has ceased. Their imaginations have not been exercised since childhood. By the time many reach the high school age, their imaginations no longer function easily. However, the theatre is a place where imagination is extremely important. Therefore, the actor's creative facilities must be kept razor sharp.

As the performer begins to develop believable characters, the technical aspects of the theatre become keys to stimulating imagination. The *stage* is a space in front of an audience that must be filled by the actor. It is a space in which ideas must be conveyed in a given amount of time. Therefore, the known factors of time and space can be useful to the actor. The performer, as a creator, must conform to time and space; so, he or she must be selective in what is to be conveyed and what is not. Not only is it necessary for the actor to imagine, but it is also necessary for the actor to make the audience imagine, too!

Imagination is not such a strange resource when it is actually used in everyday life. Whenever a situation calls for preplanning or rehearsal, imagination is used. This kind of preplanning or imagining is only a small example of how imagination is utilized when portraying a character. The actor must be someone else. The actor's responsibility is to create a character. The character must have accompanying feelings, expressions, mannerisms, and attitudes. For this task, the actor must develop imagination. The playwright does not supply everything needed to create a role. He or she gives the actor dialogue and some stage directions, but the actor must learn to analyze and interpret the thoughts of the character. The total concept of a role will be the actor's decision. The final character must be living, vital, and truthful.

Pantomime

A good way to utilize the concepts of imagination, observation, and experiences is through pantomime. *Pantomime* is defined as a sequence of facial expressions, gestures, hand operations, body positions, and movements that are taken from life. Used imaginatively by the actor, a pantomime can tell an entire story without a word being spoken. In many instances, pantomime has become

An expanded imagination and a working expertise in the field of pantomime enable an actor to create a more vivid, believable character.

so refined it has become an art form in itself. For example, Marcel Marceau and Red Skelton's pantomime sketches are very well known worldwide.

Pantomime is an extremely functional technique for the beginning and mature actor. In early development, it is used basically as an exercise to increase coordination, concentration, and control of the body. Random movements on stage are not sufficient to convey specific ideas to the audience. Pantomime will help discipline the actor to create and enrich a character portrayal. It will also help develop specific dramatic stories, locales, and atmospheres.

Stage Business

Once pantomime is taken beyond the exercise phase, it can also be used on stage along with several other techniques or "actor's helpers" to enhance the actor's performance. Another actor's helper used frequently on stage is referred to as *stage business*. This is basically the use of small body actions to convey a message. Stage business usually involves the use of properties or "props." These may include the following:

1. hand props—small objects that an actor can carry or handle on stage, such as papers, drinking glasses, dusters.
2. personal props—items on the actor's person, such as watches, eye glasses, rings.
3. costume props—any accessories used by actors on stage that relate to costume attire, such as fans, gloves, handkerchiefs, and swords.
4. Stage props—items or objects that relate to the physical scene, such as stools, pillows, and lamps.

All of these techniques and helpers are to enhance the actor's performance. They should be used to their fullest, remembering however, to keep the performance clean and concise.

26

REHEARSAL TIME

For each of the following activities, divide into groups of three to five. These exercises will give you a chance to use your imagination and to practice pantomime as each member of the group will get a chance to perform for each exercise. Every group will need enough space for a small audience and for the performer. The performances should be between 30 to 45 seconds. Try to incorporate as many of the ideas discussed in this scene and scene one as possible. While the actors are performing, the rest of the group (audience) should be making notes on the performance in their theatrical notebooks. After each performance, the audience should give short, constructive critiques of the performance. What was good about it? What could have been improved? How?

Activities

1. Select a prop from the first list, and create a scene using one of the characters from the second list. Relate the scene to your group. Try and use your imagination as much as possible, but still keep the scene believable.

Prop List
a. handkerchief
b. hair pin
c. bowling ball
d. toothpick
e. cigar
f. guitar
g. pocket watch

Character List
a. business executive
b. cook
c. nurse
d. Indian
e. mechanic
f. street-sweeper
g. Martian

2. Supply imaginary circumstances that might have led to one of the following:

a. A millionaire walking along skid row at four in the morning.
b. An infantryman in the middle of a battle eating a peanut butter sandwich.
c. A farmer having lunch at a very expensive restaurant and reading the *Wall Street Journal.*
d. A ten year old piloting a space ship.
e. A socialite carrying a gun in the middle of the desert.

Then relate your story to your group. Again, try to use your imagination as much as possible.

3. Imagine you are preparing dinner in a modern kitchen. Take your time preparing the food. See the food in front of you; determine the size of the pots and pans, the stove, the sink, the refrigerator. Use your past experiences to help visualize these things. Keep in mind what it is like to actually prepare a dinner. Make your audience see images clearly as you perform your preparation. Be specific in your body actions so your audience knows exactly what you are doing. They should be able to visualize in their minds what you are doing.

4. Create and perform a short pantomime of one of the following:

a. You are in a workshop making an object. Determine who you are and why you are making the object. Use as many tools or equipment as possible.

b. Dress yourself for a party. Although it may be any kind of party, it is very special, and you want to look your best.

c. Pick up a very heavy box and put it on a shelf. Then take it back off the shelf, open it, and find something inside.

d. Walk through an art gallery and become absorbed in a painting that depicts several people. Let one catch your eye. Slowly begin to absorb the characteristics of the person and begin to become that person.

e. You are confronted by a thief on the street. Attempt to disarm him or her.

f. You have a flat tire. Change it with difficulty.

g. Create a scene in which two people are fighting. Carry out the fight in slow motion. You should pantomime both roles.

h. You are performing a very delicate biological experiment in a laboratory with many test tubes and other scientific apparatus. It is your task to perform the last vital experiment in a long-range project. As you complete the project, a bottle of liquid spills on your notes.

CURTAIN

Scene Two has discussed the importance of a full realization of the actor's physical and mental resources. Thus, communication with the audience becomes a completely conscious task. Resources originate within the body (senses and feelings), as well as in the mind (imagination and memory). Emphasis has been placed on the importance of nonverbal behavior and accurate presentation of ideas and images.

Finally, the technique of pantomime was discussed as an important function of the actor. Pantomime improves physical coordination, accuracy in characterization, and the clarity of a story. Pantomime also helps the audience gain acceptance of the truthfulness of the stage situation.

Scene Three

VERBAL VIBRATIONS

Scenes One and Two stressed that the actor must control and direct physical responses and internal resources on stage. Scene Three will discuss another major resource of the actor—the voice. This scene deals with the voice and reading aloud on stage.

Throughout the history of the theatre, the voice of the actor has been emphasized by critics, teachers, and performers. In *The Lives of the Noble Grecians and Romans,* Plutarch stressed the importance of good diction. The eighteenth and nineteenth centuries emphasized declamation and the grandiose style of oratory. The twentieth century ushered in a trend toward naturalism and simplicity in vocal qualities. Today, the main concerns of the actor are to project the voice to the back of the theatre, to cultivate a flexible voice for the creation of character, and to speak with clear pronunciation and varied inflection.

From the Stomach

One of the first responsibilities of a beginning actor is to be heard at the back of the theatre. At the same time, the typical stage voice must have a conversational tone. The actor's words must sound as if they are being spoken for the first time. The voice must be spontaneous and natural. This means that speech cannot be slovenly and inaudible.

The voice also reveals several things about a stage character. Therefore, the need for an effective voice is most important. For example, a character's speech will reveal his or her background, education, social class, occupation, age, and emotional or physical condition. Speech, therefore, should be free from all of the actor's personal habits. Just as movement tells much about a character, speech, also, reveals many facets of a character. The actor should use this to the fullest.

Since the condition of the body also influences the voice, an actor should be in control of his or her entire body before, after, and especially during a performance.

Just as with concentration, the body should be relaxed yet alert when speaking. Anxiety and tenseness result in one's speaking too quickly. This causes a loss of clarity and variety in the voice. The habits of good speech are necessary on the professional stage. Artistic standards in the theatre are high. Excellence demands total control of the body, which helps control pronunciation and varied inflection in the voice.

Correct Breathing

Developing the voice, like anything, takes time and energy. The first step in voice development involves learning to breathe. Everyone breathes to support life in his or her body. The actor must learn to breathe correctly to support a strong voice on stage. This takes a certain type of breathing. It is called breathing from the diaphragm. Breathing from the *diaphragm* (a muscle located between the abdomen and the bottom of the rib cage) means that when a person inhales, the diaphragm contracts and flattens. At the same time, the abdominal muscles expand, forcing the ribs up and out. This enlarges the size of the chest cavity, creating a partial vacuum. Air rushes in to fill the vacuum. The air enters through the mouth and nose, goes down the trachea into the lungs, and expands them.

When a person exhales, the abdominal muscles contract, pushing the diaphragm upward and pulling the ribs in. This reduces the size of the chest cavity and compresses the lungs. The air is driven out through the trachea, past the larynx (where sounds are produced), and out of the body, through the nose and mouth.

Speech and Voice Definitions

There are several important terms used in relation to the production of sounds by the voice. Some of the more important ones for the actor are listed below:

Volume is the force of air that determines how loudly or softly a person speaks.

Range is concerned with the distance,

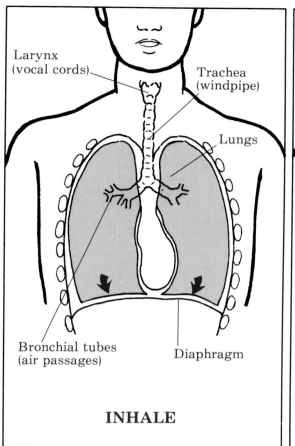

Larynx
(vocal cords)

Trachea
(windpipe)

Lungs

Bronchial tubes
(air passages)

Diaphragm

INHALE

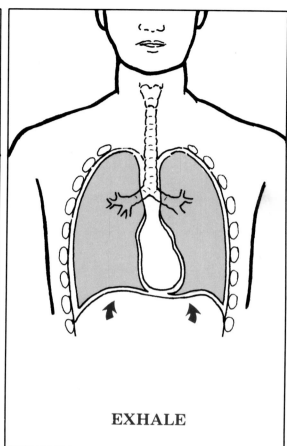

EXHALE

measured in notes, between the lowest and the highest pitch of a comfortable, effective speaking voice.

Pitch is concerned with how high or low a voice may sound. There is an optimum speaking pitch for every voice, but it can be changed through training.

Intensity involves the quality in speaking that is shown both by the speech and the manner of an individual. Intensity

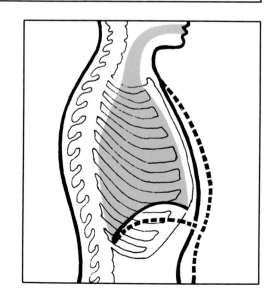

arises from strong feeling. It is not just loudness of tone. It is a controlled vocal energy that reflects emotional tension.

Inflection is the voice's rise and fall in pitch. Inflection enables a voice to show shades of feeling and meaning.

Resonance is the vibrating quality of the voice that produces an amplification of tone. Resonance depends primarily on the openness and flexibility of the cavities of the mouth and throat. This, plus the other vocal qualities, creates the *timbre* of a voice, or what makes it different from every other voice.

Pronunciation is the correct utterance of words so that vowels and consonants are given their proper sounds, and syllables are given their proper accents.

Flexibility is the ability of a voice to modulate or vary within a pleasant range of tone. A flexible voice has the following characteristics: variety of pitch and rate, inflection, pauses, emphasis, variation in volume, and differences in intensity.

Rhythm is the alteration of silence, sound, strength, and weakness in speech. Rhythm does not necessarily imply time. It is more a matter of accenting syllables. Rhythm is usually a succession of pauses and phrases, along with an alternation of strong and weak syllables within the phrases.

Rate is the speed of speaking.

Emphasis is the stress placed upon a syllable, word, group of words, or portion of a speech. It is used to denote significance in meanings.

A *pause* is a brief suspension or hesitation of the voice. Pauses are used to em- phasize ideas, indicate divisions of thought, give listeners time to grasp a point, and to whet curiosity. They also give a speaker time to establish breath control for better speech.

Poise is the self control of an actor's vocal patterns.

These definitions can be used to break down any vocal pattern into its component parts. Once these terms are put into practice, they can be used to increase the actor's flexibility in speech.

Since the voice relates closely to physical age and condition, variations in posture, poise, and physical movement will affect the voice of the character. By slowing the pace of a character, the vocal pace will start to slow at the same time. All of these qualities can be varied until the correct matching of voice to character is achieved. Thus, in perfecting a role, the actor need not completely change his or her voice, but only modulate certain features of it to fit those of the character.

Because actors tend to overlook the distance factor between the stage and audience, emphasis should always be placed on projection. Clear pronunciation is also an important factor in the relationship of actor to audience. If the audience cannot understand the actor, the character in the play is lost. A stage voice must have vitality and force. Faulty projection and pronunciation may arise from faulty breathing. Remember, breathing from the diaphragm enables the actor to control the quantity of air taken in and also helps sustain and regulate the speed of air going out. Excellence in vocal flexibility and projection comes only with time and hard work.

REHEARSAL TIME

A large work area is not needed for the following activities. These exercises can be done in a large group and each person will be working on the techniques for self improvement. It is important that particular attention be paid to the effect of each exercise on the vocal quality produced by your particular voice. It is also important to try to catalogue the effects of each exercise on your particular voice. You may need this information for the creation of a future character.

Activities

1. The first exercise is to make you aware of the correct way to breathe from the diaphragm. While standing, place both hands on your stomach, just below the rib cage. As you breathe in, you should feel your stomach and rib cage expanding. As you exhale, you should feel your stomach and rib cage contract. Keep breathing. Feel your stomach and rib cage contract and expand until this type of breathing feels easy and natural. (Note: if your shoulders go up and down as you breathe, you are doing it incorrectly. Try and keep your shoulders relaxed and let your diaphragm do the work.)

2. For the second exercise, again place your hands on your stomach and begin breathing from your diaphragm.

After you are breathing steadily and naturally, begin letting the air out of your lungs in gentle bursts. Take a deep breath and let out each burst with a "Ha!" Repeat, feeling your stomach and rib cage react. You should feel quick small contractions for each "Ha!" Repeat the same exercise, using the *h* sound before each of the vowel sounds *a, e, i, o, u.*

3. This exercise emphasizes the power of volume and its relation to air intake of the lungs. Take a deep breath. Starting very quietly, open your mouth and say "Ahhhhh," letting your voice rise in volume as you let more air out of your lungs. By the time you reach the end of your breath, you should be at your top volume. Now repeat the same exercise, starting loudly and coming back down to a whisper. You should be controlling the air intake and output at all times. The important thing is to be able to control the volume you are using! Again, repeat the exercise, taking your volume from low to high and back down again in the same breath. You will note at this point that it is important to breathe correctly in order to sustain wind for an extended period of time. Now, try to repeat the exercise at a normal volume, sustaining the sound for as long as possible on the same breath. Repeat several more times using the vowel sounds *a, e, i, o, u.*

4. Range and pitch are very closely related, for they tend to deal with each other. This exercise will test the range of your voice and will familiarize you with pitch. It is important that you try not to vary the volume of your voice during this exercise.

Find a comfortable volume and, at a comfortable rate, say the sound *ah.* Sustain the sound for a comfortable breath of air. Repeat, letting your voice go up the musical or sound scale as you let the air escape from your lungs. You should let your voice "crack" at the top of the scale. Repeat again, taking your voice down the sound scale. Don't worry; you won't be expected to sound like a trained professional singer. Now repeat going up and down the sound ladder until you have found what seems to be the top and bottom of your vocal range. You should always try to stay within this range, unless the character you are playing calls for otherwise.

5. Intensity and inflection seem also to walk hand in hand. The best performers are skilled in the use of these vocal techniques. In these exercises, you should pay particular attention to what has to be conveyed and how intensity and inflection can enhance characterization. Which words should be emphasized? Try to emphasize them in order to convey the best meaning. Practice the following short statements, which contain different tonal patterns and varieties of intensity.

a. Some days are bright, others are gloomy.
b. The pathway is smooth but narrow.
c. Why did he spend all his money?
d. Speak softly but carry a big stick.
e. Both the boys and the girls were invited to the party.
f. That university is famous in football but infamous in scholarship.

6. The following exercises will help you develop the open throat that is necessary to achieve proper resonance.

a. Relax your neck and facial muscles. Let your head sink forward until you feel it hanging heavily and unable to sink any further. Let the lower jaw sag. Roll your head gently from side to side until you feel the muscles free and flexible.

b. Relax your head sideways as far as it will go, or until you are acutely aware of its weight. Let your jaw hang heavily. Repeat to the other side.

c. Gently touch and massage your cheeks and lips with your fingertips to increase the freedom and repose of your face.

d. Relax your jaw and tongue, and open your mouth. With the head upright, let the mouth open and the jaw sag of its own weight. The tongue should be relaxed in the floor of the mouth, with the tip resting lightly against the back of the lower teeth.

e. Prepare to speak by opening the mouth and the throat. Then, keeping the open feeling of the throat, close the lips and produce the sound *mmm* as an easy hum at your middle pitch level. Think of the tone as centered in your nasal cavities, but feel the vibrations at the front of the face and in the lips. Maintain breath control while making the sound. Repeat the exercise with *n* and *ng*.

f. Repeat the previous exercise, gradually increasing both the duration of the tone and the sense of full vibration in the nose and face. Do this intently, but without strain.

From the Eyes and Script

The first requirement in reading aloud is to look at the audience. Do this as much as possible; about 75 to 80 percent of the time. This means that when reading from a script, the written passage must be practiced until it is nearly committed to memory. A good way to practice is to scan the words ahead, concentrate on the meanings expressed, and then look up and speak. At the end of the thought, look down and find the beginning of the next thought, look up, and speak again.

Of course, the actor must be very familiar with the material in order to use this technique. Using slanted lines between thoughts in the script helps to avoid losing the place. By separating the ideas in the script, it is easier to learn to speak more clearly. This is because the ideas are divided and can be expressed in concise phrases. At first it is difficult to keep from looking at the material, but like anything else, success comes with time and practice.

Eye Contact

Looking at the audience serves a variety of necessary functions. The material tends to become more of a direct presentation. The audience becomes more involved with the performer and the material. Eye contact also serves the performer as a gauge of the audience's reaction and a means of feedback from the audience on the performance. From this feedback, the actor can evaluate what aspects of the delivery need to be altered. It is also possible to determine what parts need to be expanded or deleted.

Distractions

There are many obstacles in the audience that serve as a distraction. The reader's ears must be tuned to noises in the audience: restlessness, conversations, coughing, and applause in order to correctly monitor the audience. In addition, the reader must be able to sense the effectiveness of the performance. The best way to do this is to become involved in the material and to involve the audience through the use of the techniques already discussed.

Punctuation

Sometimes an actor may be asked to read material he or she has never seen. At such times, it becomes necessary to rely heavily on punctuation in the selection. This assists in the projection of ideas. Generally, a comma denotes a brief pause. Semicolons indicate a longer pause, and the longest pauses follow a period. However, there is no substitute for understanding the ideas in a passage to express them in the best way. If material must be given with what is called a "cold" reading, it is wise to read slowly and rely on an intelligent phrasing of ideas.

Emphasizing Speech

Most beginning readers speak too fast, which usually results in a loss of meaning and attention. Generally, a good rate of delivery is about 125 to 150 words per minute. However, the rate of speaking is influenced by the number of pauses and the time used to pronounce vowels and consonant sounds. For example, some people extend the *o* in "long" and prolong the time it takes to say the word. Because the human mind can comprehend approximately 400 words per minute, an audience has spare time for thinking and is, therefore, susceptible to distraction or personal concerns.

For this reason, it is necessary that one neither dally nor rush the key ideas. The good reader uses pauses to give the audience time to think and respond, but not too much time to get distracted. It is generally good to use pauses and let the important ideas take hold of the audience, thus creating a more conducive atmosphere for interaction.

A thorough knowledge of the script and musical score enables the actor to establish a strong feeling of empathy with the audience.

REHEARSAL TIME

Each of the following exercises should be conducted in groups of two or three. Every group will need a space where they can read without being too loud and disturb other groups. In addition, each group will also need a watch or some other means to keep time. These exercises emphasize the importance of eye contact, reading rate, and clarity of phrasing. It is helpful if each exercise can be repeated several times to achieve a better effect.

Activities

1. Each reader in the group will take a turn reading the following passage of approximately 110 words. It should be read in somewhat under one minute. This is a good speed for reading aloud. Try to keep as close to one minute as possible without going over or under. The other members of the group will keep time for you. At the end of each reading, write down the exact amount of time it took you to read the passage. After several readings, see if your time improves along with your confidence in reading the passage.

I came in from camp and you from the city . . . uncertain,
apprehensive still—
having for days rehearsed, each by its own script, the play
of attitudes and words, the first tentative touch,
the implied yes
and (always) the ultimate embrace.
But as it happened: I took your hand to cross the street,
and our fingers held . . . the way vines do in growing,
and we were wonderfully inarticulate—
we were breathlessly afraid . . . like flying in a dream.
Then most of the afternoon we lay in the sun,
among the last late dandelions and curious foraging ants—
shuttling secret thoughts between us
and exquisite promises . . . anticipating evening.

Walter Benton, *Never a Greater Need*

2. For this exercise, use the same script as in exercise one, with which you now should be somewhat familiar. First, copy the excerpt as it appears on a sheet of paper. Then, take a pencil and go over the script, marking where you think there should be pauses. Remember, pauses should mark the ends of ideas or logical phrases. After you have marked your script, compare it with the other members of your small group and see how your markings compare. Why did you mark yours as you did? Did someone in the group have certain places marked that might seem more logical? Re-mark your script where you think the correct places to pause should be.

3. Finally, using the same script, gather the small group in a circle. Each member of the group will read the passage to the others, paying particular attention to eye contact. You should be able to use the markings in your script to help in the division of ideas. Each member should repeat the exercise several times until the passage and eye contact both begin to come more easily.

From the Mind

Reading aloud is an effective way for the actor to develop a good speaking voice. Oral reading, or oral interpretation, is a form of communicating directly to the audience. The object of the reader is to express ideas verbally, interpreting written words. The performer's task is to communicate an author's ideas, feelings, attitudes, and intentions to the audience as honestly and accurately as possible. Reading aloud requires training, practice, and concentration. It is also one of the best ways to perfect a performer's stage voice.

The art of oral interpretation goes far beyond this simple explanation. Its use in this text will be strictly for improvement of the actor's vocal qualities. For further information on the art of interpretation, it would benefit the actor to seek out one of the many texts on the subject. For now, interpretation will be seeking the meaning behind the script.

Concentration on Meaning

The more important the thought in a passage, the easier it is for the reader to remember. Similarly, an audience listens for ideas; it does not concentrate on

The audience's involvement in a play is as important as the actor's performance.

words alone. People, however, tend to stop listening when the material is not interesting. Most have a short attention span. Many listeners have difficulty separating important material from the unimportant. Therefore, the actor's job as a reader is to interpret and emphasize important ideas in a dramatic but logical way.

To understand the full implication of concentrating on meanings, the actor must realize that an audience has numerous emotional attitudes that adversely affect their listening ability. Therefore, the prejudices and personal concerns of the audience become of major concern to the performer. An effective voice, clear projection of ideas, and eye contact will help the actor interact with the audience and overcome their biases.

As an actor reads, the audience should become involved with the material being interpreted. This emotional involvement stems from two things: the so called defense mechanisms members of an audience bring with them, and the variety of emotional experiences the reader presents. For example, audience members might not have wanted to come to the theatre. They might have had a fight with a friend, or they may not like the material being presented. If an audience is motivated to empathize with the reader, and if the reader is performing and reaching the audience effectively, emotions can be roused in all.

A reader should remember that people perceive and react to a performance as if it were an outgrowth of themselves. Once the actor realizes this, it will be easier to understand the interaction process that stirs people's emotions.

REHEARSAL TIME

This exercise is basically an extension of the previous Rehearsal Time, but on a larger scale.

Activities

1. Each performer should choose one of the following three cuttings and perform it in front of a group of no more than ten. You should be using all of the techniques discussed in this and the previous two scenes. The final goal is to reach the audience with a *total* performance. Emphasis should be placed on each of the specific vocal techniques. Remember, eye contact is also very important for audience involvement. Your voice should project clearly and concisely to the last seat of the audience.

a. All the world's a stage,
  And all the men and women merely players:
  They have their exits and their entrances;
  And one man in his time plays many parts,
  His act being seven ages. At first the infant,
  Mewling and puking in the nurse's arms.
  Then the whining schoolboy, with his satchel
  And shining morning face, creeping like snail
  Unwillingly to school. And then the lover,
  Sighing like furnace, with a woeful ballad
  Made to his mistress' eyebrow. Then a soldier,
  Full of strange oaths, and bearded like the pard,
  Jealous in honour, sudden and quick in quarrel,
  Seeking the bubble reputation
  Even in the cannon's mouth. And then the justice,
  In fair round belly with good capon lined,
  With eyes severe and beard of formal cut,
  Full of wise saws and modern instances;
  And so he plays his part. The sixth age shifts
  Into the lean and slippered pantaloon,
  With spectacles on nose and pouch on side,
  His youthful hose, well saved, a world too wide
  For his shrunk shank; and his big manly voice,
  Turning again toward childish treble, pipes
  And whistles in his sound. Last scene of all,
  That ends this strange eventful history,
  Is second childishness and mere oblivion,
  Sans teeth, sans eyes, sans taste, sans everything.

                    Shakespeare, *As You Like It*

b. And the weaver said, "Speak to us of clothes."
  And he answered:
  "Your clothes conceal much of your beauty,
  yet they hide not the unbeautiful.
  And though you seek in garments the
  freedom of privacy you may find in them
  a harness and a chain.
  Would that you could meet the sun and
  the wind with more of your skin and less
  of your raiment,
  For the breath of life is in the sunlight
  and the hand of life is in the wind."

Some of you say, "It is the north wind
who has woven the clothes we wear."
And I say, "Ay, it was the north wind,
But shame was his loom, and the soften-
ing of the sinews was his thread.
And when his work was done he laughed
in the forest."
Forget not that modesty is for a shield
Against the eye of the unclean.
And when the unclean shall be no more,
what were modesty but a fetter and a fouling
of the mind?
And forget not that the earth delights to
feel your bare feet and the winds long to
play with your hair.

Kahlil Gibran, *The Prophet*

c. In Golden Gate Park that day
    a man and his wife were coming along
  through the enormous meadow
      which was the meadow of the world
He was wearing green suspenders
    and carrying an old beat-up flute
        in one hand
  while his wife had a bunch of grapes
            which she kept handing out
                individually
            to various squirrels
                as if each
            were a little joke
And then the two of them came on
    through the enormous meadow
  which was the meadow of the world
            and then
  at a very still spot where the trees dreamed
      and seemed to have been waiting through all time
        for them
  they sat down together on the grass.
      without looking at each other
      and ate oranges without looking at each other
        and put the peels

in a basket which they seemed
      to have brought for that purpose
   without looking at each other
And then
      he took his shirt and undershirt off
   but kept his hat on
     sideways
     and without saying anything
fell asleep under it
   And his wife just sat there looking
at the birds which flew about
   calling to each other
     in the stilly air
   as if they were questioning existence
     or trying to recall something forgotten
But then finally
   she too lay down flat
     and just lay there looking up
      at nothing
   yet fingering the old flute
     which nobody played
   and finally looking over
     at him
without any particular expression
   except a certain awful look
  of terrible depression

Lawrence Ferlinghetti, *A Coney Island of the Mind*

2. After each performance, the audience should make some constructive verbal critiques of the performance. Was the performer clearly understood? Was the performer's voice used to relate the material effectively? How could this have been improved? Did the performer use eye contact to involve the audience? Did the performer phrase ideas clearly and to the author's meaning? How could this have been improved? Did the performance come together as a whole and totally involve the group?

CURTAIN

Scene Three has concentrated on developing and expanding the range and quality of the actor's voice, the third principle tool of the actor. Knowing how the breathing process functions, understanding the various techniques of a good speaking voice, and understanding the various techniques of reading aloud are all integral parts of communication between actor and audience. The use of all these tools leads to good interaction with the audience, which adds to a good performance.

Scene Four

SETTING SCENES

Preparing to create a role on stage involves all of the actor's skill and knowledge. To make the best use of thoughts and feelings, the performer must discover how to concentrate and how to put these thoughts and feelings to work. In order to prepare for learning these new skills, the actor must develop body relaxation and control, and learn to use internal resources. These are sense, memory, observation, past experience, and imagination. Proper vocal techniques are also important parts of this process. Scene Four adds the use of improvisation to these techniques.

Environmental Stimulus

Learning to concentrate, as has been previously mentioned, can be a means by which an actor can relax. Concentration is also a process of selection. *Selection* means drawing attention to specific objects, thoughts, or activities in order to further a characterization. The two processes, relaxation and selective concentration, allow the actor to think only the thoughts and feelings of the character. They also allow the actor to respond naturally and spontaneously. When selecting reactions that seem pertinent and necessary, it is important to choose actions and words that relate to the environment specifically.

Selective Concentration

Reacting to selective stimuli also means focusing thoughts on the motivations or origins of the reactions. For example, carrying or wearing properties that relate to a character's manner or personality is simply a physical manifestation of that person's personality. A more important discovery is to find good reasons for wearing the article and why the corresponding sensory reaction results. If the character always wears a ring, the actor must study the ring in close detail and select pertinent information relating to it. It might be a gold ring with a ruby. It might be scratched beneath the surface and chipped at the rim. Further study may reveal where the character obtained the ring. Who gave the ring? Was it found? Was it bought? These details become important

The successful actor uses environmental objects and situations to enrich a characterization.

because it is through this knowledge that the actor becomes able to react truthfully.

Sometimes confusion arises as to what should be emphasized to the audience, for there are many levels of selective concentration. Each level works to fulfill the character. The most desirable focus is the character as a human being. Remember that characters on stage must be alive, vital, richly detailed in terms of habits and characteristics, and an integral part of their environment. Other levels of concentration are involved in acting a role in a play. However, primary concentration for the new theatre performer should be on the total understanding of the stage character.

Levels of Concentration

Of course, to fully understand a character, all levels of concentration must be recognized and emphasized (to some degree) throughout the play. For example, the performer may concentrate on the motivation of the character —that is, the reason a character performs a specific action.

The actor must also concentrate on the reactions of the other characters throughout the play. For instance, if a character with a sick mother complains and pleads for assistance, the objective might be to get the doctor to come to her house. The actor's concentration will thus focus on others' reactions more than on self-reaction, in this particular scene. Through concentration, the actor becomes increasingly comfortable with physical actions and with relationships with other characters.

For some roles, the playwright may require concentration on the thoughts of the character. The most desirable way to convey deep thought is to find some action that reveals the general reason for the thought. For example, by staring at a portrait, looking away, and by then staring at it again, the audience will know the character is thinking about the person in the portrait. Through concentration, the actor focuses sensory reaction or thought on the object, in this case a portrait.

Also of importance is the actor's concentration on the lines of the other actors. Listening is another art that an actor must cultivate. The response to a line must come from intense attention to the lines and not just from waiting for a cue. Good listening habits can create the illusion that responses are spontaneous and sincere.

Concern for Environment

Similar to these other forms of concentration on stimuli is the actor's concern for the environment in which the character is to be developed. The beginning actor usually performs with little concern for environment. The new performer is usually more worried about physical appearance or actions than about the physical environment. It is difficult to add this to the many levels of concentration the actor must consider. However, like all of the other factors of a good performance, the stage is another important factor with which to deal.

Rooms usually have personalities of their own, and can reveal many things about the people who live in them. A room can indicate whether a person is neat and tidy, or careless and thoughtless. Paintings might indicate a character's interest in the arts, or even that a character might have artistic bents. Papers lying around a room might reveal that a person is hard at work.

Making mental notes of every detail, color, and arrangement in a room puts an extra burden on an actor. Visualizing the entire scene before entering the stage area makes this task somewhat easier. Attention to the details of a set is part of the preparation of an actor.

REHEARSAL TIME

Each of the following exercises may be done in small groups of approximately five. You will need an area where the performer has room to move and the rest of the group can act as audience. Every member of the audience should be keeping notes on each performance in his or her rehearsal notebook. Again, these notes should be in the form of a constructive critique. What was done? Was it done effectively? How could it have been improved? What was good about it?

The actor should be concerned with concentrating on the different aspects of characterization and environment that have talked about up to this point. Play the role for creativity and reality. Try to convince the audience you are who you are playing. In addition, attempt to convince the audience you are where you are as a character.

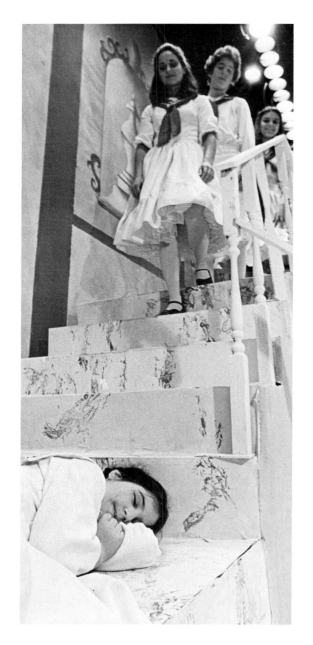

Activities

1. Perform a series of actions that could not take place anywhere but in one of the following environments:

    a. living room
    b. recreation
    c. attic
    d. garage
    e. mansion
    f. art gallery
    g. a rocket ship
    h. a movie star's dressing room
    i. a deserted house

Repeat the exercise until everyone in the group has had a turn creating an environment.

2. Create a character and an environment in which there has just been a terrible fight, and one of the characters is recovering from it. Again, repeat until each member of the group has had a chance to try creating a character with a strong emotion.

3. Now, combine two characters in the same environment to create a scene. Remember that it is important for your audience to be able to see the environment, even if it is not really there. This will take concentration on the parts of both actors involved. You should also be aware that listening to another actor is important for a feeling of spontaneity and reality to the audience. The two characters will portray one of the following situations:

    a. two children in a haunted house
    b. two lovers after their first fight in a restaurant
    c. two aged people on their front porch in the summer
    d. two executives waiting in a stuck elevator
    e. two people in an office trying for the same job
    f. two actors auditioning for the same part in a play.

4. Again, with just one actor at a time, enter a room, and have a definite attitude or emotion, such as happiness, sadness, or depression. Let the room change that attitude. Repeat, so each member of the group has a chance to perform.

Improvisational Stimulus

Improvisation means creating a very brief plot or story and implementing it with dialogue that is not planned or rehearsed. Usually, two or more actors are involved. The technique of improvisation may be used in two particular instances: (1) as a way to experiment with voice, simple characterizations, different environments, emotions, and a variety of body movements, and (2) in implementing the script when some of the original spontaneity of a character or environment is lost.

Suggestions for Improvisation

Plots for improvisations can be found in plays, or they can be created with original words and actions. Since the new actor needs to learn to "move" a scene through actions, words, and motivations, it may be more valuable to create improvisations than to rely on a story from a play. The following suggestions will implement the creation of improvisations.

1. Do not chatter aimlessly; say only what must be said. Words should make contributions to the objectives of a story.
2. Make sure the scene keeps moving by having several possible actions in mind.
3. Begin the scene at once, even though it may be independent activity. If the scene is thought about too long, it will lose spontaneity.
4. Do not work to entertain the audience. Work with the other actors by becoming sensitive to changes in their feelings and their attitudes.
5. Whenever a choice in action is confronted, make certain the action chosen is natural rather than contrived.
6. Make character preparations offstage. Go on stage knowing who, where, what, and why the character is involved.

Chain Improvisation

Improvisations are not limited to two characters. They can be performed with several characters going in and out of the improvisation at different times. This is called *chain improvisation*. A chain improvisation, while beginning the same way as a normal improvisation, causes the scene to continually expand as a new person enters the story.

These new characters either alter or perpetuate the action. This exercise requires quick thinking. It may include as many as ten actors on stage, each with his or her own objectives, characterization, and imagination. Total commitment to the scene, intense listening, and rapid adaptation are required for good chain improvisation.

Listening

The skills acquired as a result of communicating with others are applicable to the acting process. One of these, listening, evokes various responses. Listening can generate a verbal response, or simply an inner thought, or a physical reaction, such as a facial expression or a gesture. No matter what kind of response, listening involves interpreting words, meanings, or symbols. Interpreting or understanding speech also involves a reaction within the body. The reaction is often physical. The performer reacts to attitudes and thoughts either positively or negatively, through nerve endings and muscles.

The listening process involves three other kinds of responses: stimulation, evaluation, and understanding. In terms of an actor in a play, the response may come in a variety of ways, depending on the playwright.

Communication is often blocked by a lack of response due to faulty listening. Actors can never afford not to listen. The interaction provided by the playwright through the characters is the stimulus by which the life of the play proceeds. The audience can become involved in this action. The audience, too, must participate through its mental, emotional,

and physical responses to the actions, sounds, and words being presented on stage.

Most people do not take the time to examine their listening habits. Most people could also profit by paying attention to improving speech perception. One way to improve listening is to directly motivate ourselves. In other words, listening must be done on an active, conscious basis. A commitment

Improvisational techniques aid the actor in the development of specialty characters.

should be made to listening, either for personal reasons or simply through a desire to actively and consciously participate in the listening process.

Whether on the stage or in social communication, listening involves a re-

sponsibility. This is extremely important, of course, when working with other actors on stage. Each actor depends on one another for a rehearsed but spontaneous set of responses to a situation in a play.

All of the actors' energies need to be focused on the inner forces needed to project truthfulness of character. The actor needs to be alert to all cues that are given by others. Pauses enable the performer to concentrate on the main ideas. Vocal variations and body action offer meaning and feelings about what is being said. Finally, the actor must control emotional responses so that they do not distract and cause problems.

REHEARSAL TIME

The following exercises can be done in groups of approximately five or six, with two of the group as actors on stage and the rest of the group as audience. The last exercise must be done in a large group, with a minimum of six actors on stage. This will be discussed further in the actual exercise. You will need room for the actors to have freedom of movement while in the created stage area. The audience members should be keeping notes in their notebooks on the dif-

ferent aspects of the improvisations that have been discussed in the reading material. Is the action natural and believable? Does the action flow from one character to the other? Are the actors listening and responding to each other? How could the presentations have been improved? What was good about them?

Activities

1. Choose one of the situations listed and create an improvisation with

two partners. Repeat the exercise until everyone in the group has had a chance to perform.

    a. trapped in a mine
    b. performing a robbery in the middle of the day
    c. undergoing a change in personality as a result of a traumatic experience
    d. revealing each other's identities
    e. burying a pet
    f. having a snowball fight

2. Two actors agree on the where of the situation. One is on stage and the other enters. The actor already in the room must find out "what" the entering actor has done. The entering actor does not want to tell, but must be coached into telling. The actor entering the room must relate to the situation by being overpowered by "what" has just happened. After the "what" has been discovered by the actor and the audience, start with another group, change situations, and the "what" of the second actor. Repeat until everyone has participated.

3. Create improvisations in which an entire set of three words must be used to create a dramatic story. These elements must not be actually said on stage, but they must appear as elements of the dramatic action. For example, the first set of words listed could result in an improvisation about a school teacher who dreams an eraser is attacking her and calls the police for help.

    a. fantasy, eraser, telephone
    b. atom, hanger, hat
    c. documents, pipe, lipstick

    d. chair, hair, dress
    e. fingernails, table, eyes
    f. book, bracelet, closet
    g. bench, shoes, fingernail polish
    h. nylons, bow, teeth

4. This is a group chain improvisation. It will require a large space for the actors to maneuver and perform. It is best done with a large group of at least six actors going on and off the stage. The scene is a grand ball, and each of the actors should decide on a character before starting. No actor should know the identities of the other actors. Two of the group will start the scene as a butler has just served them beverages. When the actors feel they are ready, they may enter one at a time and become involved in the action. They may also exit when the action calls for it.

Try to be original and natural while still listening to what is going on and become involved as a character. The rest of the audience should be keeping a critique of the different actors as they enter and exit. Again, it is important that the critique be constructive and critical of each actor's performance.

Emotional Stimulus

Handling and controlling emotions is a difficult matter for an actor. Literally, *emotion* means *outward movement,* and thus implies an impulse toward open action. Emotions are a large part of everyday living and experience. They are primarily a safety valve that relieves tensions and anxieties.

Just as emotions serve individual needs, the emotions of a character in a play serve the character's needs. The projection of a character's emotions permits the audience to share them. Hopefully, they will empathize with the character through these emotions.

Beginning actors are often impressed with rampant emotion in a play. However, uncontrolled emotions are dangerous for the actor and destructive to the purpose of the play. For example, making an audience cry may not be a particularly effective technique, because it may become so involved that it ignores the continuing action on the stage. Only when the projection of emotion lends itself to realizing the truth of a character is emotion truly a powerful tool. Emotion should clarify the meaning and the action of a play. It should help the audience more fully experience the sensations projected on stage.

Projecting Emotions

There are many theories concerning the projection of emotion in a theatrical production. All of these theories narrow to two basic premises: (1) in order to project an emotion, the actor must experience some kind of internal physical response; (2) at the same time, the actor must project some kind of external response.

Bodily reactions experienced in daily living are a result of "giving in" to feelings. So, too, the actor must give in to physical sensations needed to express an emotion on the stage. Sadness may result in crying, because it is a release of tension. The tears are a physical, glandular response that manifest an emotional state. Because the actor is interested in truth—not reality—on stage, actual tears are not always necessary to invoke the feeling of sadness. There are other physical ways to project this feeling. For example, just staring silently at the floor can project grief. However, the actor must be physically free to approach the emotion. The body must be ready to respond to any emotional conditions that the playwright indicates. Without the physical sensations, an audience will be unable to share in the feelings of the actor. If an actor is true to emotions, the audience will empathize and feel the same emotional response.

An important physical condition for projecting an emotion is the breathing process. If an actor is tense and anxious, the breathing will be faster, and the voice will be high-pitched and awkward. Thus, if the performer can control the breathing process, emotional responses can be controlled more appropriately. In other words, emotions usually corre-

Emotional scenes sometimes pose problems for new and even experienced performers.

spond to a particular breathing pattern. Breathing has different rhythms and depth. This depends on the structure of the emotion and the energy released. If the breathing process can be controlled, the actor will be better able to move rapidly into any situation that calls for an emotional response.

Emotions are also projected on stage through physical action. In other words, the playwright specifies a whole range of actions for actors to perform. These actions must be appropriate to the characters. They must also be internally motivated. Action is always a result of something that has happened to the character. Concentrating on the cause of the emotion that produced an action, not just on performing the action to effect the emotion, is the truthful way to pro-

ject emotional behavior. If the actor thinks only of performing an action to show emotion, there is a danger of reverting to stereotyped behavior.

Words need not always accompany physical action. However, words help convey an emotion more completely. The playwright will usually provide dialogue when emotion is to be produced. In these situations, the actor must be careful not to rely solely on words to show emotion. Along with dialogue, it is important to demonstrate the feelings of the character. This is done through correct motivation and particularized physical action.

All emotions have a common characteristic; their projection always relates in some way to an external object. Sadness, anger, or any other emotion usually finds an external object or person as its desired end. In other words, when an emotion is felt, it is usually expressed to someone or something in some way.

Emotions are not manifested at random, nor do they have a beginning or an end. They are continuous and contiguous with life. Emotional responses are really continuous conditions that just "flare up" at opportune and appropriate moments in a play. Emotions are never really depleted. They lie dormant beneath the surface and emerge when they are motivated or stimulated.

Tears

Playwrights often require a character to cry or shed tears. At these moments, an inexperienced actor often becomes concerned with trying to cry. Concentrating on crying real tears frequently results in no tears and no indication of feeling. It is a misconception that an actor who is weeping has to produce real tears on stage. The majority of actors on stage must find other ways to express sorrow. By concentrating on the cause of the emotion, the physical action is induced by letting the emotions respond naturally.

A word of caution is necessary at this point. It is not wise to utilize "tricks" to create the illusion of crying. Spraying menthol fumes into the eyes, smelling an onion, or putting petroleum jelly below the eyes only produces a false situation. Also, it is not necessary for the actor to feel the real sorrow that sometimes results in tears. Correct stage activity and free physical response that relates to grief can indicate the truth of the emotion. For example, staring at a picture, or holding on to someone or something very tightly can usually project grief or unhappiness as a substitute for crying.

Laughter

Creating laughter on stage is another difficult task. As with crying, laughter is caused or is genuinely motivated by someone or something. A definite physical response must be felt.

Laughter may result from trying to hide a feeling of inferiority. A person laughs to prevent another from getting the better of him or her. Someone laughs because something is amusing or possibly embarrassing. Once the reason for laughter is discovered, the actor can laugh naturally without trying to force it. However, if laughter does not sound natural, it is better to find other ways of showing joy and happiness. For example, happiness may be demonstrated by leaping from a chair and dancing lightly around a room.

Love

Finally, a love scene is one of the most difficult experiences for a young actor. A young actor tends to be embarrassed in front of people when a kiss is needed. However, it is important to keep in mind that love scenes are a part of the business and need to be rehearsed. Usually, embraces are rehearsed at a time when only the director and a few of the actors are present. The director will coach the kiss and the various stage positions of the actors.

The best way for two actors to help each other in this situation, is by sharing the responsibility of compatibility and helping one another create a good working environment. Love between two people can be revealed by careful use of the eyes. Gazing into another actor's eyes can indicate deep emotion. In some instances, the only indication of love can be the exchange of quick glances or whispering in the other's ear. However, the most effective way to perform a love scene comes from giving full cooperation to the director and the other actor.

REHEARSAL TIME

These exercises can be done in groups of approximately five or six. Again, they will be done with two of the group as actors, and the rest as audience. After each performance, the group should give oral critiques of the performance and how it could have been improved. Also, note the strong points in the scenes and what made them strong. Each exercise will be repeated until every member of the group has a chance to participate. Keep notes in your theatrical notebooks on each performance and how certain situations could be utilized in a real play situation.

Activities

1. Choose any of the following emotions and see if you and a partner can create a scene that naturally builds upon the emotion, evoking the same feeling in the audience.

a. anger
b. fear
c. boredom
d. smugness
e. love
f. tenderness
g. greed
h. selfishness
i. indifference
j. joy
k. sadness
l. happiness
m. bravery
n. shyness
o. cowardliness
p. depression

It is not necessary for both characters to be portraying the emotion. On the contrary, often one of the characters will need to be a recipient of or respond to the other's emotion.

2. Create a scene in which two people respond emotionally different to the same situation. Make sure that while you are each reacting to the situation, you are also reacting to each other. Do your reactions to the situation change when you see the other actor's reaction? How does this affect your audience? Repeat the exercise using a different set of actors and a different situation. Repeat until all members of the group have had a chance to participate.

3. Create a scene where you are leaving a friend you might never see again. Make the circumstances of the departure clear and concise for the audience. React to the situation, and let your body relate the feelings of regret and sorrow that you should be feeling. Repeat with different characters and a different situation, until all members of the group have participated.

4. Devise actions for each of the following situations and act them out.

    a. two young children walking in a park together

    b. father and son are having a serious discussion about a dying mother

    c. two young people meet at a dance and become friends

    d. a mother shows concern for her daughter, who is going around with "undesirable" friends

    e. a boyfriend and girlfriend are moving to different towns

    f. a family is being evicted from their home because they cannot pay the rent

    g. two good friends are leaving one another to go to college

CURTAIN

    This scene has been concerned with the actor's abilities to project important aspects of a stage character. Selective concentration has been discussed as a means of narrowing thoughts, objects, and ideas for the audience. The actor has learned to select a variety of levels on which to focus inner concentration. These include the character and character motivation, other characters, various thoughts, and the dialogue to be memorized.

    Improvisation was introduced as an aid to creativity. Listening was discussed as a means of cultivating clarity of characterization, spontaneity, and believability. The concept of emotions and their projection by means of bodily symptoms and physical actions was introduced.

    Finally, the discussion of the importance of being aware of environments should give a solid foundation for the introduction of play or script analysis. This will be discussed in Act Two.

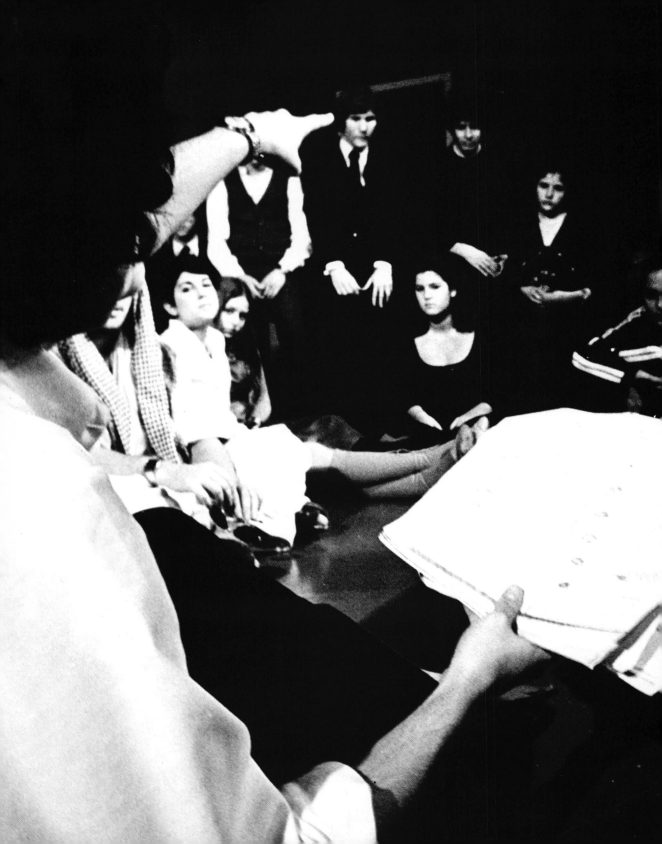

Scene One

ANALYTICAL ALTERATION

Previous discussions have centered around how the actor can discover and control the physical, vocal, and emotional potentialities of the body. In these discussions, the idea that the actor must be "true" to the actions and beliefs of the character were of primary importance. However, the actor does not operate solely within the framework of these resources. The actor is, of course, aided by the script. Therefore, the second level of development in the actor's studies focuses on the relationship between the actor and the script. This is the means by which the performer may become "truthful" to the dramatist and his or her work.

The Text

Since the play itself is a relatively bare format, consisting of words and some stage directions, the actor must approach the play and the character being portrayed with careful deliberation. The focus of the actor's study should be on the problem of bringing the play to life.

Studying Scripts

A playwright usually begins to write with an idea of developing an experience or a story. Mental images of characters, who serve as agents of the play, are formed. A particular form or aspect of life is then envisioned. When an actor studies a text, the primary responsibility is to recreate those images and transfer them to a person who is involved in living experiences. One of the most efficient and profitable ways to be true to the intention of the playwright is by thoroughly studying the script. The text of a play should be read aloud several times. This enables the actor to understand the point of view and theme of the play. It also reveals the various facets of the characters. Although some actors think they can read a script once and understand the play, careful analysis of the details will provide more of an insight into the play itself.

After the initial reading with the entire company of actors, each individual actor should reread to gain further insight into the particular facets of the character to be portrayed. In a careful reading, the actor should note all pertinent information concerning the environment in which the character lives.

The mood of each scene should also be examined. Further, the actor should analyze the background of the character's life, insofar as can be determined.

This process of evaluation by the group of actors and by the individual actor is necessary to understand the play fully. The group should reach agreement on the goals of the author. They should also agree on the motivation of individual characters. Any disagreement about the meaning of the play or the motivations of any of the characters should be revealed during the discussion sessions. In this manner, the goals for a production can be clarified and the cohesiveness of production enhanced. For example, the outcome of a production of *Othello* might be different if the director and cast choose to portray the story as a conflict of several military interests rather than as a story of excessive love and jealousy among three persons.

Determining Goals of a Play

An effective way to determine the goals of a play and the motivations for individual characters is to divide the play into the following components:

1. *Exposition:* that portion of the play that exposes the following necessary information to the audience:

   a. Locales and Time
      (The specific place and time of each scene)
   b. Characters
      (The names, types, and relationships of the characters)
   c. Antecedent Events
      (What important action has

occurred before the opening curtain?)

d. Form and Type
(Comedy? Drama? Tragedy? Melodrama? Romance? Epic? Mystery? Satire? Burlesque Farce? Fantasy? Absurd? Social drama? High comedy of manners? etc.)

2. *Point of Attack*

a. Specific Incident
(The earliest incident in the play that arouses strong audience interest and exposes the basic conflict)

b. Protagonist
(The person about whom the play is written)

c. Antagonist
(The person or force opposing the protagonist)

3. *Crisis*
The high point of suspense when a decision must be made—the turning point

4. *Climax*
The moment of highest interest for the audience—the final answer to the basic conflict (In a one-act play the crisis and climax are often the same.)

5. *Resolution or Falling Action*
Action which occurs between the climax and the final curtain.

6. *Evaluation*
Personal reaction to the theme, mood, style, dialogue, character development, plot construction, entertainment value, and literary value. (The theme is generally considered to be the idea that is basic to the thought of the play

The script is the actor's all important link to the playwright.

—the central idea being presented by the author. Usually the theme can be summarized in a sentence; for instance, "The theme of *Agamemnon* is that pride, taken to excess, leads to destruction.")

Motivation

The actor should be careful not to place *undue* emphasis on isolated, individual scenes in a play. At times, actors are required to act out isolated scenes. At these times, it is advantageous to scan an entire play for surface meaning and then concentrate solely on only one of the scenes. Also, at times, there is a tendency to rely too heavily on performing one or two moments of a scene, neglecting the play in its entirety.

Each scene must be properly projected as a whole and understood in relation to the rest of the play. Scenes are part of a complete play in which many types of relationships are taking place. In each scene in a play, the actor must continually ask why a character is performing a particular action and what effect this has on the entire play. Answers to the questions of why something is being done and what will motivate the action further must constantly be answered in order to keep the characters believable.

Idiosyncrasies of Character

The final step in analyzing the text usually comes when the actor discovers the particular idiosyncrasies of the character and attempts to translate them into physical action. This process involves a further careful reading of the script. For example, in *The Three Sisters* (by Anton Chekhov) the schoolteacher, Kulygin, has not been in the military service, whereas all the other men have served in the army, and this fact may be significant to the portrayal of Kulygin. It might mean that an actor would create a limp for Kulygin, which would pre-

clude his being subject to service in the military. He would also need to specify how the leg was injured.

It is important to characterization that actors be specific about such details and the origin of habits; otherwise, their portrayal will be less believable and complete. Because Laura, a character in Tennessee Williams' *The Glass Menagerie,* is a young crippled girl, an actress portraying Laura should begin rehearsing the play with a slight limp. At the same time, the actress must realize that her crippled condition has precipitated psychological problems, such as her shyness with people.

In studying the text of a dramatist, the actor should be ready to project certain personal facets in the character. This is an expected and natural thing to do and usually relates to correct casting.

The actor should also utilize imagination and intuition to supply expressions and moods for the stage role. Thus, the actor's own personality and features combine with imagination and intuition to provide total commitment to characterization.

Characterization

Each character in a play should be unique and individual. A *straight role* is defined as a part that is well suited for a particular individual because of age, ethnic origin, or physical characteristics. A *character role* is defined as a part that necessitates the altering of the actor's physical and perhaps psychological makeup. It may not be very difficult for a teenager to portray a twenty-year-old because the small age difference would not be a particular obstacle. However, a fifty-year old prison warden role may be more difficult for a teenager to portray because of age and unfamiliarity with the problems of such a position.

As stated previously, a character is portrayed by an actor in conjunction with personal resources and understanding of the dramatist's concept of the character. The result will be different from any other actor's conception of that same role. No two actors bring the same experience and analysis to a role. However, all actors should have similar guidelines for studying the characters they will bring to life.

Analyzing the Role

An actor may begin character analysis by asking two important questions. First, what does the character want in the play—that is, what is the character's motivating force? Second, what will the character be willing to do to get it?

Once the actor finds what motivates a character in terms of primary need, the next task is to represent this motivation by specific actions. In Arthur Miller's *Death of a Salesman,* Willy Loman wants his sons to be well liked and popular. He is willing to condone and even encourage cheating and lying to gain this end. In terms of specific action, it becomes clear that Willy rejects anyone who does not achieve popularity, including himself.

Note these examples of translating a stage character's motivation into specific actions. This is how they should be stated when an analysis is needed.

Vague: A character wants to be happy.
Specific: A character wants to be happy by performing charitable deeds with the Red Cross.
Vague: A character "hates the world."
Specific: A character hates his mother and her friends because they laugh at him.

Other analytical questions an actor may use in rehearsal include:

What does the character do for a living; to pass leisure time?
What does the character like and/or dislike?
What do the other characters in the play say about the character?
What kinds of actions are suggested by the character's lines?
What is the nature of the relationship between the character and all other characters in the play?
How does the character feel about the other characters in the play?

Character analysis becomes more complicated as the weeks of rehearsal pass, and the more penetrating questions an actor might ask about the character are listed below. By opening night, the actor should be able to answer all of them.

What does the character want out of life?

What does the character do to get it?
What does the character believe in?
What was the character's childhood like?
Does the character have any convictions? What are they?
What changes, if any, take place in the play relative to or as a result of the actions of the character?

REHEARSAL TIME

The following activities should be recorded in your theatrical notebooks. They are to be completed by each actor separately. After the analysis is prepared, however, the group may discuss different facets of the characters discovered in each play, and share information about the plays used for analysis.

A word of caution should be stated concerning character analysis. It is not the role of the actor to make value judgements on a character. It is the role of the actor to portray a character as truthfully and honestly as possible. If the actor decides the character is not good, or not something else that tends toward a judgement, he or she cannot portray the character as the character would actually be. Try to keep an analytical mind and stay unbiased and open-minded toward your character.

Activities

1. The plays listed below contain excellent opportunities to analyze plot structure and characters. (Later, these plays will provide you with acting scenes.)

Henrik Ibsen: *The Wild Duck*
Thornton Wilder: *Our Town*
Arthur Miller: *Death of a Salesman*
Tennessee Williams: *The Glass Menagerie*
The Rose Tattoo

Elmer Rice: *Street Scene*
Clifford Odets: *Golden Boy*
Eugene O'Neill: *Ah, Wilderness!*
Molière: *The Pretentious Ladies*
George Bernard Shaw: *Arms and the Man*
          Pygmalion
Anton Chekhov: *The Marriage Proposal*
Shakespeare: *Romeo and Juliet*
Maxwell Anderson: *Elizabeth the Queen*
          Winterset
Marc Connelly: *The Green Pastures*
Laurence Stallings and Maxwell Anderson: *What Price Glory?*
Carson McCullers: *The Member of the Wedding*
John Patrick: *Teahouse of the August Moon*
Jean Anouilh: *Antigone*
Arthur Kopit: *Oh Dad, Poor Dad, Momma's Hung You in the Closet and I'm Feeling So Sad*

a. Find in any one of these plays the components listed on pages 68 and 69 of this scene. Be as specific as you can.

b. Analyze, in detail, one of the characters in any one of the plays, and be sure to state the motivating desire in terms of the dramatist's conception, as well as physical characteristics and mental capabilities.

The Stimulus

Before the actor begins to act in a scene, (or an entire play) motivations for simple situations in the play must be analyzed. Each character should reveal one or many motivations. In studying a scene, some basic questions should be asked. Where was the character coming from? What was the character doing there? Why did the character leave? Why did the character come there in the first place? Is the character familiar with the room and the people in it? What is the relationship between the characters? Does the character come here often? If the character is leaving the scene, why, and to go where?

It is often necessary for an actor to utilize stimuli outside of his or her own realm of experiences for character adaptation.

Characterization and Costumes

Costumes are means by which the actor can gain added insight into a character. They permit visualization of a character in concrete terms. This increases the potential for commitment to the character. As an illustration, the use of a hairpiece may be the key to identifying with a character more fully. Or, there may be a considerable difference in the walk of someone in high heels or in tennis shoes.

The color of a costume is also important in increasing the depth of a character. Dynamic, expressive characters may wear red or other vivid colors. Meek or weak characters may wear pale colors, such as light blue or beige. Colors can help distinguish characterizations for the actor as well as for the audience.

The actor should become familiar with the character's costumes, so they can be worn as regular clothes rather than as mere theatrical accessories. For example, because most women are not used to wearing long dresses, actors in period plays should practice moving and sitting in dresses that are heavier, longer, and fuller than women are ordinarily accustomed to wearing today. If a man must wear clothes he is unfamiliar with, such as overalls or older style suits, he should rehearse in costume, until he is able to move comfortably and naturally on stage.

Sometimes, even small costuming details become distracting if the actor has not adjusted to them before the performance. If an actor is used to wearing short hair, it will take some time to become accustomed to wearing a long wig. Similarly, a moustache can be distracting to an actor who does not normally wear one. This same principle applies to accessories. Actors who use accessories should rehearse with them to become accustomed to moving with them.

Care of Costumes

Because most beginning actors are not accustomed to wearing stage costumes, they are not familiar with taking care of them. Actors must be neat and careful. Crumpling costumes on the floor after a performance can alter or destroy the appearance of a costume for the next performance. Remember to hang clothes up neatly after they are worn. Put all accessories next to the clothes. Note whether clothes need mending or ironing and make sure attention is given to the repairs. Be certain all accessories are in workable repair. All parts of the costume should be in order and ready to go for the next performance.

Other Stimuli

Along with costumes and environment, it is sometimes helpful to utilize a single word to classify the type of character being played. If, for example, a character is "lively" the actor should discover a walk that coincides with the "lively" concept. It might be that a "lively" person would rarely be inactive or sit for long periods of time. This kind of analysis allows the actor to continually probe deeper into the character.

Music

At times, music may be an important device in the discovery of a character. It is a stimulus to which most people respond. Music sometimes motivates people to create fantasies. It stirs emotions and feelings, and establishes moods. Actors should listen and freely respond to music. It may be worthwhile to interpret a musical composition by creating a scene that corresponds to the music. This exercise allows the actor to sustain a continuous flow of action.

Animals and Objects

Other kinds of stimuli for creating a character might come from watching animals. The delicate movements of a cat might be applied in the creation of a

very poised fashion model. The slow, lumbering walk of a cow might be applicable in the creation of a very fat person.

Inanimate objects may also be used for character stimulation. For example, a tall slender vase or a round wooden bowl might stimulate characterization of certain parts of a character.

Pictures

Finally, photographs and paintings are valuable for suggesting the physical characteristics to be used in creating a character. Classical and pop-art paintings, old and current magazines, and old and recent photographs may be used in aiding visualization of a character. It is advisable to create a character from textual analysis and then to select words, music, animal, object, or picture stimuli from which qualities may be abstracted.

Subtext

In some cases, the actor may find the dramatist failed to give sufficient information in the script to create a believable character. Thus it becomes the responsibility of the actor to create an imaginary background for that character. This imaginary background is commonly called the *subtext*. A case in point is a character who enters a scene with no indication of where he or she had been previously. It is the actor's task to supply the necessary information to give the character the correct motivation or proper mood. Sometimes, many years will lapse, but the dramatist has given few specifics as to what has transpired. The actor must fill in these gaps with subtext in order to fill out the character for stage presentation.

REHEARSAL TIME

For each of the following exercises, the actor should make notes in his or her theatrical notebook. An analysis of each of the following scenes through the various types of stimuli will be requested. It would be very beneficial if each of the plays was read by at least one member of the group as a basis for information for the rest of the group. The following scenes are to be analyzed through the questions that follow.

In *The Wild Duck* (by Henrik Ibsen), Hedvig is a young, loving girl whose prize possession is a wild duck. One evening her father comes home from a dinner party and forgets to give Hedvig a present. Very sensitive, Hedvig gulps back her tears and takes solace from her friend, the wild duck.

In *Our Town* (by Thornton Wilder), Emily dies, is taken to heaven, and is granted one wish. She chooses to return home on the day of her twelfth birthday.

In *Our Town,* George was Emily's high school sweetheart. They were married after high school and lived together until Emily died, at the birth of their first child. George goes to the funeral. It is raining.

In *Death of a Salesman* (by Arthur Miller), Biff (Willy's elder son) has discovered that his father has been thinking about suicide. In the basement, he finds a rubber pipe hooked to a gas line.

In *The Glass Menagerie* (by Tennessee Williams), Laura is an extremely shy crippled girl. Her only comfort is a glass menagerie which is arranged on a number of shelves in the living room. Laura enters the living room very upset. She ran away from the dinner table after having been embarrassed in front of a "gentleman caller."

In *Golden Boy* (by Clifford Odets), Joe Bonaparte has become a boxer against his father's wishes. Joe is ready to leave on a tour and his father gives him a new violin, an instrument that Joe had studied previous to his boxing career. Joe accepts the violin to avoid hurting his father, and leaves the house. After second thoughts, he returns the violin.

In *Golden Boy,* Joe Bonaparte has been boxing for about a year when his father decides to come to a fight. Mr. Bonaparte cannot go out into the audience to see the fight, but he hears the roar of the crowd at various intervals. Then he stares in the direction of the arena. He goes to the exit door. Then he goes back and again listens to the crowd.

In *Ah, Wilderness!* (by Eugene O'-Neill), Richard and Muriel have exchanged letters and arranged to meet one another after dark at a dock. Because of a misunderstanding about the place of the meeting, each one waits at the opposite end of the dock.

In *Arms and the Man* (by George Bernard Shaw), Raina is deeply in love with a soldier who, it has been reported, has performed heroic deeds. After Raina and her soldier declare their love, they decide to have lunch together. Raina quickly runs up the stairs, turns to throw her love a kiss, and goes to her room to put on her hat and cape.

In *Pygmalion* (by George Bernard Shaw), Eliza enters the house of Henry Higgins. She has never been in such a stylish living room, and begins to examine the room very closely.

In the *Marriage Proposal* (by Anton Chekhov), Lomov, a powerful and suspicious landowner, is waiting to meet Chubukov and ask him for his daughter in marriage.

In *Romeo and Juliet* (by William Shakespeare), Juliet is waiting impatiently for the return of her nurse to bring news of Romeo. She appeals to the gods to unite the lovers and bring Romeo safely to her.

In *Elizabeth the Queen* (by Maxwell Anderson), Essex has been sent by the queen to Scotland to fight in a war. Essex sits alone in his tent, reading dispatches from England, and a courier arrives from England with a message from the queen. He reads it and is dissatisfied with the message. He expected better treatment from the queen, with whom he has had a close alliance.

Activities

1. Consider and analyze each scene for the questions pertinent to analyzing any character within a scene. These questions can be found in the beginning of this section on page 73.

2. Decide on the physical characteristics of the characters in each scene and how they would affect the character.

3. Describe the costumes of the characters, and note any parts of the costume or accessories that might give the actor trouble or that might take getting used to on stage.

4. Decide what type of music might be used to describe the particular scene. Hint: What would you use as background music if you were making the scene into a movie?

5. What other physical stimuli could the actor use in each of these scenes to motivate character analysis? Animals, pictures, etc.? How could these be used?

Analysis of a role may require discovering some of the more pertinent physical and psychological elements of a stage character. These are outstanding traits that identify a particular role. It is the actor's task to project every identifying feature of the character. Usually this is achieved through physical or verbal action. In addition, every feature, whether external or internal, must be analyzed in terms of the origins of that particular behavior.

The Elements

Physical and Psychological Elements

When a play is seen or read, a physical involvement should be felt. A person's experiences and thinking are related to the stage situation. However, the performer must suppress attitudes and feelings about the character and the situation, and assume those of the character. In ancient times, the actors wore masks to adopt the external characteristics of the character. For example, in the Kubuki theatre of Japan, the actor would sit before a mirror and concentrate on the appearance of the mask and then behave accordingly. After such concentration on a grief mask, the actor would feel sad.

Today the actor does not go to the extreme of wearing a mask. Personality is expressed through external behavior, inner feelings, and attitudes. Thus, the actor's task is to discover the many facets of a stage personality and to shape that personality into a physical, vocal, and psychological life.

Each stage character is a unique individual. Some have behavior patterns foreign to our way of life. Others behave in ways typical to our society and life.

Stage characters, therefore, may have both unique and typical behavior to be interpreted. This means that the stage personality should reveal typical but significant patterns of human experience with which the audience can identify. At the same time, the character should be unique to the audience's experience.

Generally, it is not complicated to project an overt physical element, such as a limp, blink, or distinctive walk. On the other hand, it may be more difficult to project a psychological or mental character element, such as avarice or cowardice. Because the origin of these elements may not be readily apparent, the process involved in depicting a physical character element is twofold: first, discover the origin; then execute the physical element as a natural and habitual part of the character. A psychological character element must also be manifested in a visual or physical manner. However, to know how the character will externalize the element, the actor must first discover the reason for the mental characteristic. These can be found through the use of the character analysis.

Once the actor has completed an analysis and fully understands the character, the physical and psychological parts of the character must become comfortable on the actor. To do this, the actor may have to practice these traits in personal life whenever it is feasible to do so. Good acting requires daily practice, in and out of rehearsal.

Substitution

A final concept to use in presenting a more believable character portrayal is *substitution*. That is "personalizing" the character or an action on the stage. This requires replacing or substituting an emotion, feeling, or attitude with another in order to make the feeling more believable to the actor. For example, if the actor has difficulty projecting boredom, it may be possible to relate experiences in the actor's life that caused boredom to the character's boredom.

Substitutions should be as close as possible to the character's feeling. This means that the actor's experience should not be so far removed from the actual stage experience that few parallels can be drawn.

Emotion Memory

The term emotion memory was coined by one of the most famous theorists in the history of theatre, Constantin Stanislavski. His techniques have served as a model for realistic acting. Many successful actors have been schooled in his system. *Emotion memory* is defined as replacing an actor's feelings for a character's feelings through recall of these feelings. Stanislavski believed that an actor must feel genuine emotion, and this can only be accomplished through the relating of personal feelings to the character's feelings.

As a technique, emotion memory is used primarily as an exercise in preparation for creating a stage character. Few actors apply this method to actual performance situations, and those that use it too frequently are referred to as *method actors*. In fact, the term has come into some disrepute due to actors' carrying it to an extreme. The method that works for every actor will be different, but the final end should be a truthful and believable character on stage.

REHEARSAL TIME

For each of the following exercises, it will be necessary to go back to the preceding exercises on pages 77 and 78 and use the same list of scenes. This exercise should be done in a large discussion group. For each of the scenes, take turns describing the following:

Activities

1. What might be some of the psychological characteristics of the characters in the scene?

2. What might have caused these characteristics?

3. How might these psychological characteristics manifest themselves through the character?

4. What might be some substitutions that might be used to show the character's feelings during the scene. Be specific in your substitutions.

While the group is discussing, it would be a good idea to keep notes in your theatrical notebook on each of the characters and the information that is discussed. This information might come in useful when it is time to begin preparing these scenes for presentation.

CURTAIN

One of the major responsibilities of actors is to study the relationship of the actor to the written script. Therefore, it has been stressed that the actor must be truthful to the dramatist and to the work. This is achieved by making a careful analysis of the play and by focusing attention on the idiosyncrasies of the stage characters. Also important is the study of individual characterizations to identify specific motivations within characters.

Other techniques for studying characterization are: (1) discovering physical and psychological character elements; (2) visualizing the costume of the character; and (3) relating the character to relevant words, music, animals, objects, pictures, or paintings. Finally, characterization has been discussed in terms of substitution and emotion memory.

Scene Two

MAKING MOODS

The importance of discovering the motivating force of a stage character and the main action of the play have been continually stressed. Analysis of the script and characterization were the key techniques in helping to determine the vision of the playwright and the motivation of the characters. This scene will describe additional techniques used for translating the motivation of a character into specific and meaningful physical actions.

Dramatic Actions

Actions are physical expressions of needs, desires, and drives. Action does not refer solely to events as they are executed. It is also the tension that precedes an event (tension may even become an event). Usually, actions are performed on stage with a purpose or intent—an *objective*.

Specific Objectives

Once the main objective of a scene is discovered, it can be expressed in quite specific terms or actions. This leads to the expression of the objectives of an entire play. These goals should also be expressed in a specific way. This means that the long range goals of a character that bear on the play must also be expressed in specific and clear terms. Specific objectives for a character will motivate the actor to perform definite physical actions on stage that will, in turn, allow his or her energy to be channeled properly.

If at times, even though motivation is specific and immediate, the actor cannot think of the proper actions to achieve the goal, the actor might ask, "What would *I* do in similar circumstances?" The details of the scene must then be analyzed. The actor will provide circumstances that will enrich the characterization. Then a series of actions that will satisfy the desires of the character must be visualized. If the actor sees the action as a series of *beats,* defined as units of action, personal experiences can then be more freely applied to the situation. Once personal experience is used on some of the beats, specific action can be created, thus giving direction to the scene.

A further note might be added to the technique of establishing specific objectives. In order to find or invent adequate motivation for an action, the actor must be genuinely interested in the objective. In other words, there must be a commitment to the action. This commitment is what generates believability.

In performing physical actions, it is often difficult to know whether motivation is clear. Usually the director or acting instructor can tell that clear motivation is or is not present.

The concept of dramatic action is defined by Richard Boleslavsky, in *Acting the First Six Lessons* as that "which the writer expresses in words, having that action as the purpose and goals of his words, and which the actor performs, or acts, as the word itself implies."

Action has a shape of its own. It begins at a certain point. It develops and progresses in a particular direction. It grows in complexity, and it increases in tension until a climax is reached. This

The superior actor is able to portray a large variety of emotions and dramatic situations.

kind of action depends on clarity of performance. It is important that the actor be prepared for it by understanding the process that precedes every action. The performer should not be concerned about reaching the major action at the end of the play. Rather, concentration should be made on so-called smaller actions, which, in turn, reveal the interpretation of the play moment-by-moment or beat-by-beat. This approach will channel small actions to the major action at the end of the play.

Dramatic action also implies heightened action. This is action that is intense. An action can be heightened or made larger than life by performing it with urgency and importance.

The actor should be aware of these primary factors that add suspense and theatricalism to acting. At the same time, these techniques keep the action moving. In essence, all action requires some measure of urgency and importance. (Even boredom must be presented with interest; it should not be boring in its presentation.) The actor should use emotion, memory, observation, imagination, and other techniques to convey urgency and importance.

Levels of Characterization

Dramatic action cannot be described simply as surface action. The actor must also examine the thought and feeling that underlie this kind of action. When building a character, the creation takes four specific forms: (1) physical traits, which can be described in the stage directions, in the play itself, or by other characters; (2) social traits, which relate to the environment and to the people surrounding the character in the play; (3) psychological traits; and (4) moral traits, which are both a result of the character's thoughts and feelings, consciously or unconsciously expressed.

All of these different levels of characterization contribute to the dramatic actions that are performed in terms of the objectives revealed by a character. They also contribute to the goals that are achieved (or not achieved.) Each character responds to a given action according to the physical, social, psychological, and moral orientation of that personality. Each level can be an environment for dramatic activity. The manner of a character's response will heighten the action and give an active expression of personality.

85

REHEARSAL TIME

For each of the following scenes, it will be necessary to have an area that can be used as a stage for performance. These exercises are best performed if the actors have a short period of time prior to performance to rehearse the scene. However, too much rehearsal will stop the spontaneity, so only a short amount of time is needed to establish basic motives and to set up the scene.

Activities

1. After each of the scenes has been performed once, a discussion of the different performances with constructive criticism would be advantageous. Try to repeat the same scenes with the same actors after the critiques and watch for improvements in performance. Again, it would be good to re-critique and point out improvements. Keep notes in your theatrical notebooks on how each scene

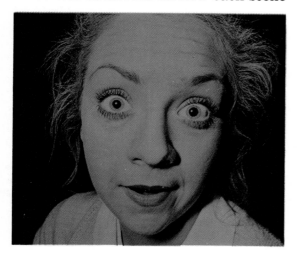

built tension and how different techniques were used to achieve this tension. Perform the following scenes so as to emphasize dramatic intensity and urgency. If needed, try breaking the scene into beats as previously described.

a. On a quiet, weekday afternoon you and your neighbors are going about your business, cleaning house, washing clothes, shopping, shining shoes, gossiping with neighbors, talking on the phone, etc. Then, in the middle of the street, a young man stabs a girl. Everyone in the building looks on but no one interferes.

b. As you enter a strange room and start to cross it, you become aware of a unique sound and come to a dead stop. At first you are frightened; you do not move. Then you realize that a small animal is making the noise. You are relieved and feel a little silly. After the tension is gone, finish walking across the room.

c. You have come to visit your grandfather in the hospital for the last time; he is very sick and is slipping toward death very quickly. Enter the hospital room carefully, slowly close the door, and visit for a few minutes with your grandfather. He cannot speak, and can only faintly hear your voice.

d. Two girls (or boys) meet for the first time after having heard about one another from a mutual friend. Both discover that neither likes the other. Then perform the scene by discovering that you like one another.

e. You suspect that someone in your group (military unit, classroom, social club) is stealing money from the members. In a meeting, you reveal this suspicion and indicate that you know who it is. The group reacts with suspicion and distaste.

f. You have fifteen minutes to put your house in order, and leave for the airport to catch a plane. The phone rings; you have a visitor; you begin to drop items; and you repack your suitcase. It is doubtful you will make your plane.

g. You arrive at the train station to meet your parents, whom you have not seen in ten years. You are early and thus have time to become anxious and nervous. As other friends of your parents arrive, you feel uncomfortable.

h. A group of people begins to gather in an airport, all of them waiting for the same flight. The plane is late, and there is talk that it will never arrive. The plane lands and you gather your suitcases together. A few minutes later there is another announcement, that the flight has been canceled and rescheduled for the following day.

i. A department store opens at 9:30 A.M. and a large group has gathered outside because there is a close-out sale. The doors open and the shoppers rush into the store and quickly begin to go through the merchandise.

j. The bus you take home every night is moderately crowded, but you are one of the first people to board it after work. Tonight the bus is very crowded, with people standing packed in the aisles and becoming rude and irritated. Slowly, people make their way through the crowd to get off at their respective stops. The improvisation ends when the last person leaves the bus.

k. You and your wife (husband) have been traveling across the country by car. For hundreds of miles there has been no sign of a motel, but finally you come upon an old motel. You enter the office and meet an old man, who shows you to your room. The room is musty and dirty, and you tactfully try to tell the man that you would rather keep driving because you have decided you do not need sleep.

l. Housewives are confronted by door-to-door salesmen who are usually persistent and high pressured. A typical housewife, you are trying to be polite by telling a salesman you are not interested in purchasing a new vacuum cleaner.

Dramatic Scenes

Sometimes an actor may be required to play a role in which the character has to make a decision between two fairly equal alternatives. Yet, how will the audience know what the character is doing if the dramatist has not written dialogue to that effect?

Ambivalence

The answer is that ambivalence may be seen by an audience in physical actions the character displays on stage. The actor may pace, frown and appear pensive, consult books, draw from a deck of cards, or do any number of actions to project the idea that a difficult decision is in the making, one that is causing ambivalent feelings.

The actor can show that a decision has been made by finalizing the action in a specific manner. To convey a decision to the audience, a playing card may be drawn, a head nodded affirmatively, or a telephone call may be made. All of this invented action, indicating deliberation toward a decision, could precede the telephone call and the dialogue written by the playwright, thereby heightening theatrical tension by emphasizing the ambivalence preceding the decision.

Drunkenness

One of the most difficult conditions for an actor to simulate is drunkenness, which must be carefully handled. Actors too often rely on stereotyped actions to convey drunkenness, for example, shaky legs and slurred speech. Again, the key to correct execution is penetrating, specific, and individualized character analysis. If the character is an extremely witty and verbal person, drunkenness may cause silence. If the character is shy, drunkenness may cause aggressive and hostile actions. There are many degrees of drunkenness, and therefore, many ways in which to portray it. Observation of actual persons, careful analysis, and a shrewd imagination can overcome this difficult acting challenge.

Insanity

Insanity, too, has many variations. Not all insane people scream or stand silent in a corner for hours. Indeed, insane people have their sane moments. Often they are insane, only when they are fearful. In all cases, the actor should find the "logic" of the insanity. Then the performer should portray the physical actions that indicate the particular insanity of the character. The constant emotional insecurity of being insane need not always be stressed. Find the origin and reveal the specifics that have led to the insanity.

For example, in Eugene O'Neill's one-act play *Ile,* the captain's wife goes insane and is required to play wildly on the organ. An actress who plays this part should interrupt this action, at intervals, with stares, sighs, and pauses, rather than obsessively belaboring the organ-playing. Her insanity will thus be particularized and specific.

Reminiscence Scenes

Sometimes, if the playwright writes a scene in which a character is required

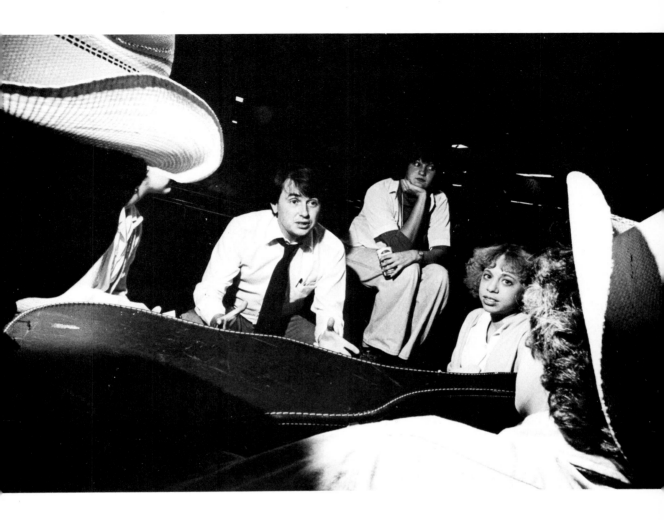

Through cooperation between the director and the cast, difficult scenes often become easier to handle.

to verbally recall past experiences or events, such a scene may involve stopping the "present" action on stage to permit the character create a nostalgic moment. There may, however, be difficulty in a scene of reminiscence if the actor becomes lost in the mood of the past. The actor cannot over indulge in the emotion of the past to the exclusion of the action of the present. To avoid this, the actor must find a reason in the present for reminiscing. For example, if the playwright has an actor gaze out the window into warm sunshine while speaking of time past, the actor may decide the motivation for reminiscing was that this warm, sunny day recalled happier times. Therefore, the lines of reminiscence remain within the present action of the play. Thus, physical reaction establishes the fact that the present is invoking the memories about the past.

For each of the following exercises, it will again be necessary to have an area adequate for performing short scenes. Pick one of the following scenes from each category and perform it using the techniques of character analysis and motivation. Try to make it as believable as possible. If it is necessary, remember you can break it down into beats and use past experiences that might help with character development. As each performer is giving his or her portrayal, take notes on techniques that you might be able to use in portraying each of the different types of moods. After several scenes, it might be advisable to give constructive critiques so that the performers might improve on their next performance.

Activities

Ambivalence

1. You want to call your best friend and apologize for starting a quarrel but are having a difficult time finding the courage to pick up the telephone.

2. You are sitting across the room from someone you think you know and cannot make up your mind whether you should reacquaint yourself with the person.

3. A company employee has threatened to expose a secret of yours unless you give him some money. Perform a series of actions which indicate your ambivalence.

4. Create an improvisation in which a group of people is at a party. Everyone in the room is extremely shy and no one seems to be able to get the party going. As soon as the party begins to come alive end the improvisation.

5. You have been called to the scene of an emergency. A man is standing on a ledge, ready to jump to his death, and refuses to talk or to listen to anyone. What are you going to do to get him off the ledge?

Drunkenness

1. You are at a social gathering, drinking quietly with a group of people. You do not usually drink to excess, yet tonight you feel the liquor is going to your head.

2. For the most part, you are a very shy, retiring person; you do not talk too much, or ask too many questions, or go out socially. It is Christmas Eve and you are attending the office party.

3. Usually you are the life of the party; however, tonight you have many things on your mind and drinking has made you very sad.

4. Perform a series of physical actions that indicate a drunken condition for one of the following people:

a. a businessperson
b. a maid
c. a housewife
d. a musician
e. a socialite
f. a bartender
g. a barber
h. a butler
i. a bank teller

5. You are a very important person in the community. At a gathering of some of the local politicians, you find that you have had too much to drink.

6. You have been invited to play bridge with a new bridge group. You want to make a good impression, but the liquor is making you become silly.

Insanity

1. Your telephone has been ringing throughout the night, and every time you pick it up the person on the other end hangs up. Build this scene slowly, until you reach a point of near insanity.

2. You are in prison, condemned to die early next morning. The night is long and the waiting seems interminable. As time approaches for you to be taken before the firing squad, you slowly go insane.

3. Sometimes the death of someone you love leaves you almost "mad" with grief. Create a scene in which you receive news of the death of someone you love and perform a series of physical actions which indicate temporary insanity.

4. You are in a dark room and a robber has bound you and locked the door. You manage to untie your hands and feet but you cannot get out of the room. Reveal a sense of frustration bordering on insanity.

5. Your plane has crashed, and when you regain consciousness you find out that you are the only survivor. The desert stretches before you, endless in all directions. You start walking, without hope that you will survive or be found.

Reveal a desperation that is indicative of insanity.

6. For months you have been aware that your family is trying to have you committed to an institution. You know you are not insane, but your family is trying to prove that you are. One night at dinner it becomes evident that your family has convinced the doctor that you should be taken to the institution tomorrow. Work out a series of reactions to prove that you are not insane; however, the family may react differently to your actions. Be certain, then, that the actions may be subject to multiple interpretations.

Reminiscence

1. You and your old high school friends are playing cards. One of you is reminded of an incident that happened in the past. You start to reminisce.

2. Five years after your husband died, you accidently come upon one of his old love letters to you.

3. Your wife sends you to the attic to clean out your army footlocker, which is full of remembrances of your army days.

4. It is time to give your daughter your wedding dress and veil, and you begin to remember your own wedding day as you prepare the dress for its second wearing.

5. Your old high school football team is playing in your town and it is the first time you've seen the school colors in twenty-five years. You bring your family to the game on Saturday afternoon.

6. After twenty years, you finally re-visit your home town. You find that nothing has changed.

Dramatic Timing

Rhythm

Rhythm refers to orderly changes and to the patterns of different beats, pauses, or actions in a play. Rhythm, as a stage quality, is difficult to define to the satisfaction of many actors and directors. Perhaps an explanatory distinction can be made between the rhythm and the terms pace and tempo, which are closely related, and also combine to contribute to rhythm.

Pace

Pace, which describes the rhythm's speech and movement patterns of each moment of a play, is the audience's concept of time. The ultimate goal for an audience, is that it have no sense of time during a play. Although this is not always the case, the audience's sense of the moment-to-moment speed of a play and the actor's sense of that speed may be different. Actor's may utilize a fast pace by hurrying over dull passages or passing quickly from one interesting point to another. They can go faster or slower to better maintain audience interest. At any given moment, emphasis may be placed on a movement, thought, spectacle, character, or speech to increase or decrease the pace of a play.

Tempo

Tempo means the rate at which a play is performed. Thus, as with pace, tempo is another time concept. Beginning actors are usually surprised to discover that performance time in a play varies little from night to night. It is usually a mistake to speed the tempo of a play from performance to performance. Rapidity of movement or speech usually results in a decrease or altering of both pace and tempo. The term slow or fast are relative in the theatre. A play usually seems to go faster as the play progresses. It actually does not increase in speed; the audience perceives an increase because they become familiar with the characters and situations. What the actor and the audience are indicating is an awareness of pace, of which tempo is a direct result.

Rhythm, which includes both tempo and pace, is denoted by changes of action, by heightened or lessened intensity or emotional variety of actions on stage. Rhythm provides emphasis by contrast in the form of accented beats of action of the play. Contrasts in speech patterns also provide emphasis and rhythm. Actors often describe rhythm as a *vertical* quality (changes in intensity) rather than as a *horizontal* quality (changes of speed along a straight line.)

Each character in a play has a rhythm, which is expressed in changes of emotions and feelings through physical attitudes. This kind of rhythm is tied to the emotional condition of the character. This will help to recreate expressions with greater clarity.

There is also a rhythm in speaking on stage that helps support the meaning of the lines by giving them proper emphasis. Analyzing rhythm in poetry requires special terminology and techniques, and highly particularized study when performing in verse plays. Rhythm in prose is similar to that of poetry in that it is established by alternating stressed and unstressed syllables as they appear in units of speech. A beat can usually be identified in prose by (1) punctuation, such as commas, periods, and dashes; (2) underlying meanings, which are not separated by punctuation but guide the actor in breathing; or (3) longer pauses, indicated by semicolons or colons; (4) periods, question marks, or exclamation marks, which separate long sentences or phrases and indicate still longer pauses; or (5) long paragraphs that have their own rhythm.

There are many possibilities within a rhythmic structure. If there is confusion as to which pattern to create, the choice should be determined by the meaning of a line and an evaluation of its components. Also, the actor must always be aware of the particular needs of the character and the situation and of the emotion to be projected.

Often the dramatic impact behind a line is not in the words themselves, but in the way they are said.

Timing

Timing is the relationship between two words, a word and an action, or two actions. Timing does not necessarily correlate with pace or tempo, which are speed factors. It is basically a coordination factor between two things. Pace can have a bearing on timing by influencing how rapidly or slowly the coordination is managed, such as fast linking of a vocal delivery to a hand gesture, as opposed to slow linking.

There are many ways in which an actor can utilize timing. Several of these ways are demonstrated in the following scene.

In act 3 of *The Importance of Being Earnest,* Jack discovers the circumstances of his birth

Jack. (Who has been listening attentively.) But where did you deposit the handbag?
Miss Prism. Do not ask me, Mr. Worthing.
Jack. Miss Prism, this is a matter of no small importance to me. I insist on knowing where you deposited the handbag that contained that infant.
Miss Prism. I left it in the cloak-room of one of the larger railway stations in London.
Jack. What railway station?
Miss Prism. (Quite crushed.) Victoria. The Brighton line. (Sinks into a chair.)
Jack. I must retire to my room for a moment. Gwendolen, wait here for me.
Gwendolen. If you are not too long, I will wait here for you all my life. (Exit Jack in great excitement.) (Enter Jack with a handbag of black leather in his hand.)
Jack. (Rushing over to Miss Prism.) Is this the hand bag, Miss Prism? Examine it carefully before you speak. The happiness of more than one life depends on your answer.

This is the finale of the play and the turning point for all the characters involved in the action. The four significant gestures for this dialogue are Miss Prism's helplessness as she sinks into a chair, Jack's exit, his re-entrance, and his rushing to Miss Prism.

Each gesture should be made to emphasize a point. The first action (Miss Prism's) indicates the emotional state of the woman, which cannot be expressed in words adequately. Jack's exit reveals his excitement and absorption in discovering the facts of his birth. What motivates him to leave the room so abruptly is Miss Prism's admission of the truth. The final actions taken by Jack are performed without words: he re-enters the room with the handbag and rushes over to Miss Prism before he speaks. These actions, performed without dialogue, reveal Jack's discovery and confirmation of the facts of his birth. If the actor who plays Jack were to rush into the room speaking lines, the heightened effect of that moment would be lost.

95

The following exercises should be experienced in small groups of five or six. Each member or set of two members should prepare several of the exercises and perform them in front of the small group. The audience portion of the small group will make notes in their rehearsal notebooks during the performances and give constructive critiques after the performance. Another group will then perform and the procedure will be repeated. After each member of the group has performed, repeat the exercise using another scene from each member.

Activities

1. Rehearse the scene from *The Importance of Being Earnest* (act 2) that begins with Cecily advancing to meet Gwendolen and saying, "Pray let me introduce myself to you. My name is Cecily Cardew."

    a. Perform this scene by emphasizing the rhythms of both characters.

    b. Discover in each of the speeches various points in which the playwright builds the dialogue to a climax.

    c. After you have familiarized yourself with the dialogue of the scene, plot a series of actions that correspond to the climactic parts of the dialogue.

2. Rehearse the scene from *The Skin of Our Teeth* (act 3) that begins with Sabina coming home from the war. Continue the scene with the confrontation of Sabina and Henry, then with Henry and Mr. Antrobus.

    a. Perform these scenes by emphasizing the rhythms of all three characters.

    b. Discover various points in each of the speeches in which the playwright builds the dialogue to a climax.

    c. Plot a series of actions that correspond to the climactic parts of the dialogue.

3. In act 2, scene 6 of *Mister Roberts* the strong personalities of the captain and Mister Roberts are shown in conflict. Build this scene by paying special attention to the rhythm of each character (i.e., the heightening and lessening of intensity).

4. Gillian is a character in *Bell, Book, and Candle* whose personality does not change significantly throughout the play. However, there are moments when she reveals herself with greater intensity and emotional involvement. Perform the scene between Gillian and Shep that begins act 2 and ends with the ringing of the doorbell. Discover Gillian's rhythm in this scene.

5. Perform the following sequence from Shaw's *Arms and the Man,* act 3. Pay close attention to the stage directions to discover what changes in character are revealed by these directions. Time the actions as effectively as possible, and avoid any gesture that would destroy the intent of the playwright.

BLUNTSCHLI. (Making a wry face.) Do you like gratitude? I don't. If pity is akin to love, gratitude is akin to the other thing.

RAINA. Gratitude! (Turning on him.) If you are incapable of gratitude you are incapable of any noble sentiment. Even animals are grateful. Oh, I see now exactly what you think of me! You were not surprised to hear me lie. To you it was something I probably did every day—every hour. That is how men think of women. (She walks up the room melodramatically.)

BLUNTSCHLI. (dubiously.) There's reason in everything. You said you'd told only two lies in your whole life. Dear young lady: isn't that rather a short allowance? I'm quite a straightforward man myself; but it wouldn't last me a whole morning.

RAINA. (Staring haughtily at him.) Do you know, sir, that you are insulting me?

BLUNTSCHLI. I can't help it. When you get into that noble attitude and speak in that thrilling voice, I admire you; but I find it impossible to believe a single word you say.

RAINA. (Superbly). Captain Bluntschli!

BLUNTSCHLI. (Unmoved.) Yes?

RAINA. (Coming a little towards him, as if she could not believe her senses.) Do you mean what you said just now? Do you *know* what you said just now?

BLUNTSCHLI. I do.

RAINA. (Gasping.) I! I!!! (She points to herself incredulously, meaning "I, Raina Petkoff, tell lies!" (He meets her gaze unflinchingly. She suddenly sits down beside him, and adds, with a complete change of manner from the heroic to the familiar.) How did you find me out?

BLUNTSCHLI. (Promptly.) Instinct, dear young lady. Instinct, and experience of the world.

RAINA. (Wonderingly.) Do you know you are the first man I ever met who did not take me seriously?

6. Perform act 7, scene 2 of the *Merchant of Venice* and discover appropriate actions to accompany Portia's description of her suitors. Concentrate on timing your actions accurately in order to enhance the thought. Work out appropriate actions for Merissa.

7. At the end of act 2 of *All My Sons* there is a very powerful scene in which Chris discovers that his father had sent defective parts to companies that manufactured planes for the war. Perform the scene. Follow the stage directions given by the playwright and add any appropriate actions that will enhance the thought and emotion of the scene. Concentrate on accurate timing of the gestures.

8. Act 1, scene 1 of *Beyond the Horizon* establishes the relationship between the brothers Andres and Robert. Most of the character of the two brothers is revealed in the physical action indicated by the playwright in the stage directions. Perform the scene (to the entrance of Ruth) without concentrating on the gestures in the script. Then rehearse the scene and pay close attention to the movements and the appropriate timing relative to the dialogue.

CURTAIN

The actor must be able to master complex stage actions and motivations, such as playing ambivalence, drunkenness, insanity, and reminiscent scenes. Furthermore, the actor must be able to prepare stage actions accurately and completely. Because the performer has to become intricately associated with the scenes being presented, the concepts of dramatic action, rhythm, and timing have been reviewed. This will help the actor more accurately portray stage characters and remain true to the intentions of the author.

Scene One

ENERGETIC EXPANSION

Act Three of this book is aimed at developing the more complex acting theories, thereby penetrating further into the stage character. This includes various ways to give a character greater dimension and believability. There are also additional ways to use nonintellectual or nontechnical approaches to the development of a stage character.

Expanding Stage Character

A number of concepts for the analysis of a stage character have already been discussed earlier in the book. The following concepts should widen the actor's interpretive abilities and advance acting skills.

The Subtext

The idea of creating imaginary backgrounds for roles when the scripts provided insufficient information has been reviewed earlier in this book. As noted, another way of referring to this technique is to say that the actor created a subtext for the character. There is a great variety of opinion as to what the subtext should accomplish for the actor. Since interpretations are many, this text will focus on how to create a subtext and will leave the individual's use to their discretion.

When an actor thinks or writes a subtext, usually a number of decisions about the character have to be made. These are not difficult when playing a major role since such characters speak many lines and several stage directions are generally offered by the playwright. Unfortunately, a playwright usually provides fewer lines and directions for the minor roles. In these instances, the subtext technique should be freely used to create a character.

The creation of subtext can begin by looking for small clues about special mannerisms. For example, Roday, a minor character in Chekhov's *The Three Sisters,* is a member of a military brigade stationed somewhere in the Russian countryside at the turn of the nineteenth century. His first lines reveal that he is the leader of the gymnastics team for the local boys. An actor who plays Roday may, therefore, infer the following: (1) Roday might walk fast, since he follows a physical fitness routine; (2) he might be a muscular man, with a loud voice and graceful, physical gestures; (3) he may stand and sit very erect; (4) his clothes might fit him well, but not in a restricted manner.

On occasion, an actor who is to play a minor role might utilize a pet phrase from the dialogue as the basis of a vivid speech pattern, which in turn may provide a stimulus for creating subtext. In *The Three Sisters,* the minor character Solony often repeats the phrase "Quick as a flash, the bear made a dash." The tone with which he speaks this line may be a key to his character. Because the line is unusual and provocative, it lends itself to creating a vivid speech pattern. Thus, an actor may come to understand the close relationship between the viciousness in Solony's nature and the viciousness of a bear. And thus a meaningful subtext results.

A stage direction that mentions a cluttered bureau might be a clue to the physical condition of the home of a character or even the character's appearance. Thus, a helpful subtext can also result from studying stage directions. In short, if a character's speech or stage directions indicate that a person has been standing all day, the actor may create a subtext of a very tiresome, boring, workday routine.

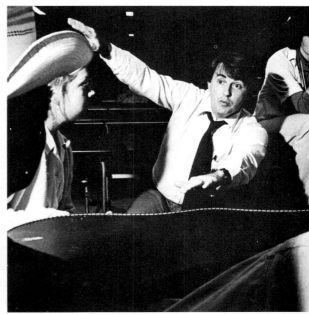

The director's relationship to the actors is often the difference between a mediocre and an outstanding performance. Teamwork is the key word.

The actor may find that another character can be a clue to discovering subtext information. For example, a character may say to another, "You look mad enough to kill somebody," which may be a clue that the actor should look angry. Meaningful subtext can then be created to motivate an angry look.

Frequently, actors who play minor characters feel that they have insufficient time on stage to establish a believable characterization of proper dimension. However, they fail to consider that every character who appears on stage, no matter how brief the appearance, can make a valuable contribution to a scene or an entire play. Creating a subtext, of course can aid this contribution.

Sources Beyond the Script

The actor who studies a script closely usually discovers a need for additional information relative to the character and to the play as a whole. Such sources as pertinent newspapers, magazines, and books will stimulate the actor's imagination and encourage thought about the locale, setting, and dress of a play. Understanding current social events and major issues of the day will also add or lend believability to a character.

Other plays, short stories, and novels by the playwright should be studied for supporting ideas. If the actor is studying the part of Tchebutykin, an army doctor in *The Three Sisters,* additional insight into the character may be gained through other works of this author. The actor would see more of the types of people Chekhov created, and especially doctors, which might initiate creative analysis relative to Tchebutykin.

It may also be helpful to study some of the important skills of playwrighting. By examining the craft of the playwright, a knowledge may be gained as to how suspense is built, how conflict is established between two characters, and how dialogue reveals information about a character. Examination will also show why some plays are considered weak and some are considered strong.

Play Structure

The following terms are associated with the structure of a play. Their origin may be found in *The Poetics* of the ancient Greek scholar, Aristotle. These terms will help with analysis of the play, which in turn will will help with character development.

1. *Plot.* This term must not be used to mean merely the summary of happenings or incidents in a play. The latter are part of a plot, but only a small part. Plot is the overall, organizing part of drama; it is the shaping part, the form-giving part. Plot in a play may be likened to architecture in a build-

ing, and that is why we call plot the architectonic part. Plot is a story *organized* in such a way as to make effective the ends and aims desired. Plot is the most highly formal part of drama; and there can be no drama without a plot.

a. *Suffering,* a technical term, will be misunderstood as merely the endurance of, or submission to, pain, loss, grief, and similar experiences. It means undergoing or experiencing any emotion or feeling—whatever happens within a character. It includes joy and rejoicing as well as misery, remorse, and physical pain. It includes the emotional effect of one personality upon another. It is clear, therefore, that this is the basic, primary material out of which plot and drama are made.

b. *Discovery* is any finding out, revelation, or making known, clear, and apparent something that was previously unknown or unrecognized. Discovery covers the entire gamut, from the mere naming of one character to another (and hence to the audience) to its highest and most important form, which is self-discovery—a personality's coming to know and understand itself. Thus it is a change from ignorance to knowledge.

c. *Reversal* is a change in the flow of action. One of the best known examples of reversal in comedy is the "tables turned" situation. Every complex plot has a major reversal, but simple plots may only have minor reversals.

2. *Character* is, first of all, the sum and substance of all that differentiates one human being from another. It is that which gives individual and separate personality to a person. It is the basic personality that is inherited and/or acquired through experience, that is, one's attitude. If limited to this level, a character could not have an important function in dramatic action, could not play a really active role in a plot. Many minor characteristics are differentiated in plots, however, on this level.

Something more is needed for an agent to become an active character, who must be moved or stirred by feeling and emotion. If the emotional impulsion is sufficiently strong and continuous, it will cause the character to think and form a desire, so that conflict arises, and the character must make a choice, must come to a decision and exercise will. When this happens, dramatic action occurs, even though the exercise of the will be merely an outpouring of grief, anger, hate, or the like in words. In this sense, then, dramatic character is, in its most formal aspect, choice or decision.

In plays involving a defined external conflict, it is possible to divide the agents into sympathetic and antipathetic. The *sympathetic* includes the protagonist, the hero or heroine (or both), and allies. The *antipathetic* includes the antagonist.

In the great tragedies, and usually in the great comedies (certainly in Shakespeare's major romantic comedies), the hero or protagonist is the initiator of the action and is, up to the reversal, the moving agent. In melodrama, on the other hand, the antagonist or villain is often the initiator of the action and the instigator of continued action. That is why the villains are often the most interesting characters. It is helpful, in determining the nature of a character and his or her function, to state as precisely as possible what the character desires.

3. *Thought.* Character in its highest form and most formal sense, is *decision* and *choice,* and the *material immediately underlying* character is *thought,* which overlays *emotion.* However, dramatic thought is emotionally motivated. It may consist of an equal combination of the intellectual and the emotional, or there may be different degrees of both. Here, deliberative thought is not in itself dramatic; thought is shown in all that the characters say when proving or disproving a particular point or enunciating a universal proposition.

The universal proposition is not a cold, logical argument (if a play is to be dramatic); the argument is highly emotional, particularly if the matter is of great importance to the characters. Therefore thought that underlies character must be emotional and intellectual. It must move people to action.

Dramatic thought makes up the dramatic argument of a play. The major dramatic question stems from the dramatic argument. Theatrically speaking, once the major question is answered, the argument is proved. For example, the major dramatic question in *King Lear* is will Lear discover the error he has made in rejecting Cordelia, and will he become reconciled with her? This stems from the dramatic argument that parents should be selfless enough to recognize true, unselfish, filial love in their children. This example is, of course, oversimplification of the overall argument of a great play and might well be misinterpreted. Thought includes the emotional and intellectual activity of the characters—as well as the overall argument of the whole play—what the play as a complete play says.

4. *Diction* or *discourse* is the formal combination of words into meaningful patterns and all that is included in the art of combining words into meaningful patterns. Discourse, then, includes the art of writing stage directions and descriptions, as well as dialogue.

Although in drama, the dialogue is by far the most important part of the discourse.

5. *Music* is any rhythmic and melodic combination of sounds, or in some instances a mere rhythmic combination. The beat of the drum in O'Neill's *Emperor Jones* is music. The speech melody of an actor speaking lines is also music. In its most formal sense, it means the instrumental or vocal music in a play.

6. *Spectacle* is used by many people in a very restricted modern sense to mean something unusual and notable that is exhibited. Therefore, a spectacle would be a kind of garish display. That, however, is not its proper meaning. Technically, spectacle is an integral part of drama—that which is visible (sometimes also audible) to the audience. Thus, costume, scenery, lighting, a mob noise off

Edmund Kean, an English actor, expressed the ideal of the volatile, romantic temperament. He brought about a radical change in the style of acting in the early 1800s. He is famous for his portrayals of Richard III, Iago, Othello, Macbeth, Barabbas, and Sir Giles Overreach.

stage, the stage business of a fight, and the movement and gesture of characters on stage are all spectacles.

The Paradox of Acting

To what extent does the actor "feel" or "become" the part? How much personal identity should be exposed to the audience? How much objectivity should be used? Writers of the nineteenth and early twentieth centuries have generally agreed that an actor should move the emotions of the audience without necessarily being moved with the audience; hence the so-called paradox. Further, these writers believed that the actor should not "become" the character being portrayed. The actor should retain some personal identity and all possible objectivity.

To exemplify this point, the actor need only examine the careers of the great nineteenth century actor and actress Edmund Kean and Sarah Bernhardt. Kean became psychologically unbalanced and could not distinguish between his stage roles and his own personality. Bernhardt had similar problems. Such extremes are relevant to the paradox concept and should be avoided. The actor's task is not to "become" a part. It is to create a believable *illusion* of being the stage character. The paradox must be that the actor *appears* to be the character but in fact is not.

Stanislavski wanted his actors to be natural to the point of almost totally uniting their personalities with those of their characters. However, he did not advocate this to the extreme of losing artistic control and objectivity. Therefore, Stanislavski's approach is oriented to in-

Sarah Bernhardt, a French actress, pictured here in her famous role as Hamlet (1899), was renowned for her golden voice. Oscar Wilde called her "the divine Sarah," a designation by which she became universally known. She was an accomplished painter, sculptor, and also wrote several plays in which she appeared.

tensive internal work on the part of the actor. Conversely, some actors concentrate on the external appearance of their characters and are always conscious of themselves as actors while on stage. Unlike Stanislavski, they do not try to merge their own personalities with their roles. They concentrate on an external approach.

Most actors, however, would agree that awareness of both the external and internal characterizations are important in creating a role. Hence, the actor has a dual personality: that of the character being portrayed and that of the actor, which interprets the significance of what the stage character is doing and saying. The study of acting as detailed in Acts One and Two has emphasized the latter role of the actor by focusing on the intellectual and technical execution of a role.

There is, however, an intangible element that may be utilized in creating a role on stage. External skills, techniques, and actions do not necessarily create art since art is usually considered to be a combination of external skills and what may be called creative forces. These forces include empathy, sympathy, imitation, and identification.

Empathy is the ability to feel the feelings of others. In the theatrical sense, it is feeling the feelings of the character. The word empathy literally means "in-feeling" and when an actor is put in the part of a character, the experiences of the character become part of the actor.

Empathizing with a person sometimes also means agreeing with them. This agreement is *sympathy.* Although sympathy is not always a necessary in-gredient of empathy, the response may occur.

Empathy also involves *imitating* the physical actions of the character. This is generally thought to be a superficial process, but it lets the actor get closer to the character in terms of external portrayal. Many actors, such as Sir Laurence Olivier, rely on heavily projecting the externals of a character but still retain a great amount of the character's believability.

Finally, there is the creative inner force known as *identification,* which enables actors to alter their personalities and become strongly influenced by the characters they play. This means the actor must have a deep respect for both the actor's and the character's identities. This mutual respect enables the actor to relate to the character in terms of similarities and differences.

Part of the identification process involves the full use of the five senses, which allows the actor to establish even the innermost responses of the character. The actor may be able to understand and reveal a mysterious "inner reality" to the audience. An illustration of this intangible quality occurs in *The Three Sisters,* when Masha reacts to "mysterious" or "intangible" forces. At moments like these, an actor may find it impossible to rely on his or her feelings and senses to identify with and capture the mystery of the moment.

In one instance, Masha hears the wind howling in the chimney and remembers that she heard the very same sound just before her father died. This memory stirs and creates the mysterious mood of the moment. In another instance, Masha speaks about her faith or belief in a universe of stars and planets; she cannot articulate it, but senses it.

There is an intuitive quality in both moments and little or no intellectual insight. Masha simply knows or senses, and identifies with the mystery of the moment. The reaction cannot be convincingly intellectualized or externalized because it is so intangible and ethereal. It is difficult to project by mere verbalization or action. For such moments, the actress must project feeling rather than ideas or physical actions. There is no certain way to achieve such projection. It can come only from experience, dedication, sensitivity, study, and application of some of the techniques discussed in this text.

REHEARSAL TIME

The following exercises could either be performed by a single actor or in groups. Try and do as many of the exercises as possible, because it is important that an actor reads as many plays as possible and also gets background in the analysis of these plays. Keep notes in your theatrical notebook and be able to discuss the decisions you made in relation to each of the analyses.

Read and study the following plays (or as many as feasible) paying special attention to their structure.

Shakespeare: *Julius Caesar*
   Macbeth
John Osborne: *Look Back in Anger*
Molière: *The Misanthrope*
Henrik Ibsen: *A Doll's House*
George Bernard Shaw: *Candida*
   Saint Joan
Tennessee Williams: *A Streetcar Named Desire*
   Summer and Smoke
Eugene O'Neill: *Mourning Becomes Electra*
   Emperor Jones
   Long Day's Journey into Night

Clifford Odets: *Awake and Sing!*
William Saroyan: *The Time of Your Life*
Arthur Miller: *The Crucible*
   The Price
   A View from the Bridge
   Death of a Salesman
William Inge: *Bus Stop*
Frances Goodrich and Albert Hackett: *The Diary of Anne Frank*
Gerhart Hauptmann: *The Weavers*
Caroline Francke and Edward Streeter: *Father of the Bride*
Jean Anouilh: *Time Remembered*
   Becket
Friedrick Dürrenmatt: *The Visit*
Tom Stoppard: *Rosencrantz and Gildenstern Are Dead*
Harold Pinter: *The Birthday Party*
Edward Albee: *Who's Afraid of Virginia Woolf?*
   A Delicate Balance

Activities

1. Create subtexts for the following minor characters:
   a. Mary Warren in *The Crucible*
   b. Mrs. Linde in *A Doll's House*
   c. Porter in *Macbeth*
   d. Flavius in *Julius Caesar*
   e. Portia in *Julius Caesar*
   f. Rosa in *Summer and Smoke*
   g. Sam Feinschreiber in *Awake and Sing!*
   h. Willie in *The Time of Your Life*
   i. Anna in *The Time of Your Life*
   j. Grace in *Bus Stop*
   k. Chuck in *Hatful of Rain*
   l. August or Anna in *The Weavers*
   m. The inquisitor in *Saint Joan*
   n. Mrs. Pulitzki in *Father of the Bride*
2. Examine the following plays to discover what additional sources could be consulted to more fully understand the background of the plays and characters:
   a. *The Misanthrope*
   b. *A Doll's House*
   c. *Saint Joan*
   d. *Mourning Becomes Electra*
   e. *The Crucible*
   f. *Macbeth*
   g. *The Diary of Anne Frank*
   h. *The Weavers*
   i. *Julius Caesar*
3. Examine *The Emperor Jones* for the contribution that music makes to the play.
4. *The Time of Your Life* takes place in a bar on one of the piers in San Francisco. Examine the play and describe the spectacle within the framework of the play.
5. Compare the dialogue in *A Doll's House* and *Mourning Becomes*

Electra. How are the two plays similar in their dialogue? How are they different?

6. Describe the suffering of Hennie in *Awake and Sing!*, of Joan in *Saint Joan,* of Nora in *A Doll's House,* of Elizabeth Proctor in *The Crucible.*

7. What is the key reversal in Molière's *The Misanthrope?*

8. Describe the major discoveries of the following characters:
   a. Nora in *A Doll's House*
   b. Brutus in *Julius Caesar*
   c. Marchbanks in *Candida*
   d. Anne in *The Diary of Anne Frank*
   e. Alma in *Summer and Smoke*
   f. Alceste in *The Misanthrope*
   g. Lavinna in *Mourning Becomes Electra*

9. Analyze the major dramatic question in the following plays:
   a. *Macbeth*
   b. *Julius Caesar*
   c. *The Weavers*
   d. *Mourning Becomes Electra*
   e. *Saint Joan*
   f. *Candida*
   g. *Awake and Sing*
   h. *The Crucible*
   i. *The Visit*
   j. *Emperor Jones*

10. Analyze the decisions and choices (thought) the following characters must make:
   a. Nora in *A Doll's House*
   b. Brutus in *Julius Caesar*
   c. Abigail in *The Crucible*
   d. John in *Summer and Smoke*
   e. Jimmy in *Look Back in Anger*
   f. Banquo in *Macbeth*
   g. Cassius in *Julius Caesar*
   h. Cherie in *Bus Stop*
   i. Brutus in *The Emperor Jones*
   j. Eddie in *View from the Bridge*

CURTAIN

Several advanced techniques that will give the stage character a greater degree of believability have been discussed. If selected to play a minor character in a play, creating a subtext will enable the actor to develop the character more fully. The actor may also want to explore sources beyond the script, such as newspapers, magazines, and books that pertain to the period.

One of the best ways to obtain a better understanding of a character is to analyze the structure of the play from the playwright's point of view.

Finally, the actor may want to work with certain inner forces through means of empathy, sympathy, imitation, and identification. This work will permit involvement with the characters through sensual and often intangible forces.

Scene Two

PERFECTING PERFORMANCE

Various techniques have been discussed by which an actor can expand and develop a stage character. Concentration has been directed to refining these techniques and filling spare hours by analyzing plays and rehearsing scenes.

These activities are aimed at perfecting acting skills. Now that this information has been covered, it becomes important to become knowledgeable of the events that lead up to and comprise the actual production of a play.

Auditions and Blocking

Auditions are one of the functions of the director. The actor's participation in auditions is restricted to reading for a part or parts.

Suggestions for Auditions

Some valuable suggestions in connection with reading for a part include the following:

1. It is helpful to read the play before auditions.
2. If interested in a particular part, it can be helpful to have practiced the speeches prior to the formal reading. However, it is not usually wise to commit such speeches to memory because of the tendency to "set" a conception that may not coincide with the view of the director. Furthermore, memorizing a part prior to the tryouts may appear presumptious and might alienate colleagues and the director.
3. Exercise careful discipline and courtesy at auditions. Be particularly attentive to all directions and requests.
4. Listen carefully to the readings by others. It may be beneficial to hear the various interpretations of your colleagues.
5. Do not strive for perfection but be flexible, cooperative, and pleasant. The key to good auditions is clear intelligent reading. Do not force emotions because they may

Auditions are often rigorous and nerve-racking, but they are necessary in order to select the best cast possible.

appear artificial. If the director asks for a highly emotive reading, provide it within the range of naturalness and comfort.
6. After casting, try to be understanding and cheerful, whether cast or not.

The Meaning of the Entire Play

After the casting of a play, it is the task of a company of actors to read and analyze the central meaning of a play. The approach to these discussion sessions should be free and flexible. Everyone in the acting company should understand the roles in relation to the total script and to each other character in the play. There does not have to be complete agreement or understanding of the play or the characterizations. Indeed, if everyone is in total agreement, discussions may be too limited, leaving no room for new ideas or theories. Gradually the company will begin to see the goals of the production in terms of the concepts desired by the actors and the director. Everything will fit together satisfactorily if the ideas are not forced or unreasonably extreme.

Finally, analyzing a play is not a terminal procedure. It does not end after the first week of rehearsal. The director and actors will be constantly conferring, adding new ideas, deleting various concepts, and building characterizations. Although the formal discussion sessions might come to a stop after a time, the actor must continually explore the play and discover it anew.

Blocking the Play

Once the overall vision of the play has been interpreted, the director *blocks* or establishes the movements and positions of the actors on stage. The setting is explained along with the location of entrances and exits, the placement of furniture, and any special features in the play. The actor should be careful to note all the details of a scene and relate them to the character being played.

Each director has a different approach to blocking a play. Because blocking is a form of expression of the play's content and the physical, psychological, and emotional levels of character, movements should be a shared experience between the director and the actors. The director may note certain movements from a previously arranged plan. These may create some necessary stage business and specific points of emphasis such as pauses and noises. However, when an actor is being blocked on stage, creativity is tempered, and the responses of the character may begin to suffer. Therefore, it is best to work in a give-and-take atmosphere with the director. A too rigid plan lessens the opportunities to improvise and develop characterization.

While blocking is proceeding on stage, the actor should be determining the motivation for all movements. As stated previously, a character should not speak or perform a physical action unless there is a reason for doing so. Therefore, it may take from four to six weeks on concentrated rehearsal before true character motivation can be achieved.

Because of the long hours required for a fairly mechanical process, patience and cooperation between the director and cast is necessary during the important, but often tiring process of blocking. Just remember that good blocking will serve to make "work rehearsals" more exciting and easier for the development of characterization.

Blocking Terminology

Following is a list of terminology that will be useful when going through the blocking process. The director may have additional terms that are used for blocking a specific play.

Ad lib. From the Latin *ad libitum* ("at pleasure"), the term applies to lines supplied by the actor wherever they may be lacking in the script but desired in the production.

Aside. A line on stage, directed to the audience, which is not supposed to be heard by anyone except the audience.

Build. An increase in speed or volume in order to reach a climactic theatrical moment.

Cue. The last word or words of a speech, or the end of an action, that indicates the time for another actor to speak or act.

Drop. The dropping of volume on the last word or words of a speech.

Pick-up cue. A direction given to actors to avoid undesirable time lapses between lines or action.

Top. This term indicates that a line is delivered with more volume or intensity than the line or lines preceding it.

Marking the script. When an actor is given directions for physical movements on stage, he or she records all these moves and positions in the margins of his or her script. The following are some of the most commonly used notations:

X. Cross (stage).

XC. Cross Center (stage).

XDL. Cross down left (stage).

XDR. Cross down right (stage), (*XUL, XUR, XC, XDC,* etc.)

A *downward arrow* may indicate "sit" and an *upward arrow* "rise."

Example of a Prompt Book

X to W.S.

MASHA. I am not talking about my husband. I'm used to him, but among the civilians generally there

X to desk chair

are so many people who are crude and *unfriendly* and haven't any *manners.* *Rudeness* upsets me and

Sit on desk chair

offends me. I suffer when I see that a man is not fine enough, gentle enough, polite. When I happen to be among the teachers, my husband's colleagues, I'm simply miserable.

Standing by sofa

VERSHININ. Yes . . . But it seems to me it's all the same whether they are civilian or military, they are equally uninteresting, at any rate in this town they are. It's all the same! If you listen to one of the local intelligentsia--civilian or military--what you hear is that he's worn out with his wife, worn out with his home, worn out with his estate, worn out with his horses . . . A Russian is quite supremely given to lofty ways in thought, but will you tell me why it is that in life he strikes so low? Why?

MASHA. *Why?* — Taking off gloves, while Xing to window, drops gloves on chair

VERSHININ. Why is he worn out with his children, worn out with his wife? And why are the wife and the children worn out with him?

MASHA. You are not in a very good humor today.

VERSHININ. Perhaps. I haven't had any dinner today, nothing to eat since morning. One of my daughters is not very well, and when my girls are ailing, I am seized with anxiety, and my conscience torments me for their having such a mother. Oh, if you'd seen her today! What a miserable wretch! We began to quarrel at seven o'clock in the morning, and at nine I slammed the door and went out. (A pause.) I never speak of it, and strangely enough I complain just to you. (Kissing her hand.) Don't be angry with me. But for you alone, I'd not have anybody--nobody . . . (A pause.) *Pacing twice* *X to Masha*

in front of Vershinin, off UC *X up to level, look at UR.*

MASHA. What a noise in the stove! At home, just before Father died, it was howling in the chimney. There, just like that! *Turn to V.*

VERSHININ. Are you superstitious?

MASHA. Yes. *Stepping off level*

VERSHININ. That's strange. (Kissing her hand.) *X to her* You are a magnificent, wonderful woman. Magnificent, wonderful! It is dark here, but I see the sparkle of your eyes. *X to love seat*

MASHA. (Moving to another chair.) It's lighter here.

VERSHININ. I love, love, love . . . Love your eyes, your gestures, I see them in my dreams . . . Magnificent, wonderful woman! *Xing down with her* *By left ear*

Look at candle on desk MASHA. (*Laughing quietly.*) When you talk to me like that, for some reason or other, I laugh, though I'm frightened. Don't do it again, I beg you . . . (In a low voice.) But talk, though, it's *Lean on arm of love seat with hand on head* all the same to me. (Covering her face with her hands.) It's all the same to me. They're coming here--talk about something else . . . *Rise, X DL*

Pick up gloves on chair

121

REHEARSAL TIME

For each of the exercises in this section of the book, you will use the same set of plays that are listed below. A group of actors will be chosen for each play and will go through the actual process of creating a play.

One-Act Plays
Anton Chekhov: *The Boor*
J. M. Synge: *Riders to the Sea*
W. W. Jacobs: *The Monkey's Paw*
J. M. Barrie: *The Twelve-Pound Look*
August Strindberg: *Miss Julie*
Serafin and Joaquin Alvarez Quintero: *A Sunny Morning*
Stanley Houghton: *The Dear Departed*
Philip Moeller: *Helena's Husband*
Alice Gerstenberg: *Overtones*
Eugene O'Neill: *In the Zone*
Irwin Shaw: *Bury the Dead*
Lucille Fletcher: *Sorry, Wrong Number*
Stephen Vincent Benet: *The Devil and Daniel Webster*
Susan Glaspell: *Trifles*
Oliphant Down: *The Maker of Dreams*
Terence Rattigan: *The Browning Version*

Activity

1. In this first step, you will be required to select and read the play, and with the other actors and one member of the group designated as the director, work out the blocking and mark your scripts.

Memorizing Lines and Rehearsal

During blocking and the execution and completion of stage movements, the actor should begin to probe or analyze the stage character in depth. Usually this will begin by exploring personal resources and experiences as they relate to the stage character. Sometimes this will begin by studying and observing other people. Often, imagination is the beginning of a subtext for a character. At the same time, inventing stage business will reveal the inner emotions and motivation of the character at specific and important moments of the play. During rehearsal, the actor should decide on the overt manner and physical appearance of the character. Establishing manner, appearance, and stage business is generally a cooperative effort of both the actor and director.

Specific Characters

Studying a specific character also involves interpreting lines of dialogue. The actor has the responsibility to determine the meaning of lines as they relate to the stage character and to the central idea of the play.

To determine how lines relate to a stage character, it is once again necessary to discover the motivation underlying the lines. The actor must first ask; "In what context did the character speak the line, especially in the concept of the line preceding it? How does this relate to the overall objective of the character?"

It is necessary to recognize the real significance of a line does not lie in the mere information it gives the audience. The actor should be concerned primarily with the underlying intent of a line, that is, the reason the character speaks the line. If there is difficulty in discovering this intent, the actor may benefit from transferring the thought into some concept of concrete action. For example, Hamlet's "To be or not to be" may be paraphrased very simply as "To live or not to live." The action implied by this line may be suicide; Hamlet's decision to kill himself or not to kill himself. The specific action of the line may then be related to the overall objective of the stage character. Although Hamlet is contemplating suicide at the particular moment he speaks the line, he is also involved with the larger objective relating to the entire play: avenging his father's death by killing King Claudius. If the actor discovers the motivations underlying all of the lines and the relation of those lines and their subsequent actions to the meaning of the entire play, the task of understanding the major intent of the dramatist should be near completion.

Memorizing Lines

While studying the underlying intent of actions, the actor should also be memorizing lines. There are no set ways to memorize lines, no hard and fast rules. Some actors pace up and down in a room as they memorize. Some actors cannot memorize unless another person is listening and reading the lines of other characters. Some actors can memorize only while actually rehearsing on stage. No matter the method or the role, memorizing lines is not easy. However, the director can help ease the process.

Before memorizing lines, the actor should discuss with the director the various interpretations of the lines. In this way, a relationship will be made between memory and cohesive, meaningful interpretation. Hence, it is possible to learn the "whole" even while learning the parts. It may be helpful to learn blocking prior to memorizing lines, so that lines and movements will be coordinated on stage. Whenever possible, lines should be associated with the action that is taking place on stage. In this way, motivation and meaning will then be reinforced.

When memorizing lines it is also important to begin adding any vocal pattern that may be necessary for the character. In this way, the vocal pattern will become engrained along with the lines and their meaning.

Again, there is no "one way" or "special way" to memorize lines. Each actor must determine an individual method that works best. Most directors prefer that actors memorize lines as quickly as possible. This will take intensive study and repetition, but it is a must for best results during rehearsals. It is generally considered good practice to have lines memorized no later than the third week of rehearsals. After that, the actor should be able to rehearse without a script in hand. This frees the actor to experiment with hand props, movement, timing, interpretation, and motivation.

Technical Adjustments

In the last two weeks of a play, the director generally pays closest attention to the technical aspects of producing the play. Sets, costumes, and lights are adjusted according to the instructions of the director. Characters may wish to alter minor points of blocking or utilize different hand props. Furniture may be rearranged. The director may move a scene to a different part of the stage for better illumination. Sound may be added for greater emphasis. The timing of the play may be altered because of physical difficulties that slow the action more than the director anticipated.

This period of technical adjustments is crucial for actors. Momentarily, great attention is directed toward the external details of the play. Little attention is paid to character analysis and line interpretation. During the last two weeks of the rehearsal period, the actor should continually establish the believability of the character.

Although it may be difficult to maintain the spontaneity of the character because the performance may get boring and uninteresting after several weeks, the actor must make the role continually interesting and exciting for the audience. One way to do this is to perform improvisations, which can provide surprise and spontaneity, at warmup rehearsals. This will enhance body and vocal flexibility. Actual performances should also have some of these believable, spontaneous, true-to-life qualities.

During rehearsals it is necessary to give the director and technical crews full attention and courtesy. With full cooperation from the entire cast and crew, a good production can be achieved. Therefore, it is necessary that there should be no behavior that would diminish the total performance from either the actors or the technical crew.

Final Dress Rehearsal

One of the most exciting events of the rehearsal period is the final dress rehearsal. It has heightened importance because it marks both an end and a beginning; the end of rehearsals and the beginning of performances before an audience. Nervousness is usually intense as the atmosphere teems with activity and tension. Everyone desires to perform to perfection.

However, a final dress rehearsal can often be a technical disaster. Actors may forget lines and movements; lights and sound effects may go awry; scenery may fall and costumes may tear.

The director is aware that such "catastrophies" will occur, and that they are not necessarily of major importance. The final dress rehearsal should be viewed as a means of getting out the "kinks" of a production. While everything can go wrong, there need be no stigma of failure. Theatre professionals have even said that a bad dress rehearsal can mean a good opening performance.

REHEARSAL TIME

Activity

1. Now that you have read about rehearsals and have a blocked script, which you have read and discussed within your group, go through the rehearsal techniques. Memorize your respective lines. Go through blocking and rehearsing for a final performance as the goal. Be cooperative with your director and learn your part well. You are working toward a final performance in front of peers, who will be critiquing you.

The Performance

Opening night usually finds the actor in a high state of nervous excitement. However, once on stage, all tension should be channeled into deliberate, concentrated energy which will allow the actor to combine skills and creativity.

The run of a play varies according to each situation: a high school production may run one or two nights. College productions run anywhere from three to seven performances. Community theatre productions may run anywhere from one to five performances, and in professional theatre, a play may run anywhere from one night to two years. Regardless of the length of time in each situation, actors have a similar problem; how can they keep their performance spontaneous and alive?

Performing every night for an extended period can easily tempt the actor to relax and rely mainly on a mechanical execution of the role. This soon takes on the appearance of rote activity and results in the loss of momentum and excitement in the characterization. To guard against giving a static performance, the actor should continually rejuvenate the character with some of the techniques used during rehearsal periods; re-establishing the objectives, rereading the play, performing improvisations that elicit spontaneity, and concentrating on off stage preparation.

If the play has a long run, the director may meet the problem of tedium by letting the actors make changes in minor physical actions. Changes in physical action, though not apparent to the audience, may be the key to revitalizing a performance.

Dedication

Every person who performs in a play, whether amateur (unpaid) or professional (paid), should develop a dedicated attitude that permeates a well-executed production. Simply stated, being dedicated means that the actor has a total commitment to the play and the production.

The many hours of work are rewarded with the satisfaction of an audience-pleasing performance.

Cooperation, courtesy, punctuality, thoroughness, and personal thoughtfulness combine to make the so-called professionalism, or dedication to the theatre. If a director says cues are slow in being picked up, it should be remedied by the next rehearsal or performance. When the stage manager says "five minutes to curtain," actors should be ready for their entrances. All actors should be at the theatre at the time designated by the director. This applies to both a rehearsal and a performance. Make-up should be carefully applied, and as the director designates. Because even small problems, such as facial tissues strewn around the make-up room can be annoying to others, good personal hygiene is also essential in the theatre, where people work together closely in a restricted space. In other words, in every facet of the theatre, again, there must be a dedication to the play and to the rest of the cast, crew, and the director in order to perform to the fullest and bring off a good production.

REHEARSAL TIME

In the preceding activities you have read, discussed, blocked, memorized lines, rehearsed, and are now ready for the performance. This final exercise would best be done in a theatre if possible, or in a large room where there is ample space for the actors to play out their parts. This is the culmination of all of the work done in this section of the book.

Activity

1. While each play is being presented, the rest of the acting group should be taking notes on all of the facets of the play and its actors, and should be ready to discuss the play and its production at the end. Remember, one of the things all actors like is to know that their efforts have been appreciated. Let them know at the end of the production with a good round of applause.

CURTAIN

Preparation for producing a play in front of a live audience involves extensive rehearsal periods in which actors study the meaning of the play, block the play, and study the specific characters. The last two weeks of the rehearsal period centers around making technical adjustments germane to producing the play. During this time, actors need to concentrate on keeping "in character" on and off the set.

When rehearsal is completed and the performance of a play begins, actors need to adhere to a routine in which their stage characters are continually rejuvenated. Theatre discipline also includes a dedicated attitude that commits actors to cooperation, courtesy, punctuality, thoroughness, and personal neatness and cleanliness.

Scene Three

STYLISTIC STANCE

Thus far, various techniques and concepts concerned with projecting a character on the stage have been studied. Acting exercises that implement these techniques and concepts have been based on the actor's personal experiences and on contemporary plays. On several occasions, reading and analysis of plays from other periods, such as those of Shakespeare, Moliere, Chekhov, and Ibsen, have been used for different purposes. However, none of their characters were required to be recreated. Actors, therefore, must be able to develop many different styles of acting to keep pace with the trends of drama. Many of these plays are being recreated every day, and the actor should be ready to play the different parts.

Style and Historical Periods of Theatre

Style is defined as the means by which the truth of any particular play is represented. A theatrical style approaches a play through the study of its particular period. By understanding the cultures and mores of the period, the actor can understand the circumstances under which the play was originally produced. In a more restricted sense, style is any process that reflects the mood of a particular period.

One way to take on the style of a particular period is to become saturated in the study of the period. The country, its people, its theatre, and its playwrights all are important in the study of historical plays. Again, it is important to remember that the main concern in a play is to present the characters in a truthful and believable manner, and this cannot be done by study alone. The actor must begin to feel an affinity for a character whether contemporary or historical.

Complexities of Style

Although seemingly paradoxical, the historical period of a play is not always a sure indication of the required style of acting. For example, we tend to think of Renaissance plays as overdrawn portrayals of life with unrealistic poetic language, or that all Greek plays are rather rigid and formal. Actually, however, Renaissance plays often require a very realistic acting style, and *Hamlet* often plays best when the verse is broken with pauses and delivered in an undeclamatory manner, such as is used in most modern plays. Conversely, some contemporary plays should be acted in a formal and somewhat unrealistic style. Because *Winterset,* a modern play by Maxwell Anderson about New York slums and gangsters, is written in blank verse, actors usually adopt a style of delivery that is more formal than that of contemporary speech.

A contrast in acting styles can be seen more clearly by comparing a fifth-century (B.C.) Greek play by Sophocles and a French seventeenth-century play by Molière. In *Oedipus,* the acting style should resemble the style of the ancient Greeks, who favored formalized verse, large movements, and large masks, and cared little about either human or personal details and costuming. On the other hand, *Les Précieuses Ricidules* "The Pretentious Ladies", a play about aristocratic ladies and gentlemen in the reign of Louis XIV, requires that actors pay close attention to human and personal characteristics and such things as drinking tea and using fans. Thus, acting styles are flexible both within historical periods and throughout history.

Period Manners and Customs

Of the many sources that reveal the manners and customs of a particular period, historical books, diaries, and biographies are particularly valuable. In the seventeenth century, for example, gentlemen frequently took a pinch of snuff, and this may signify a period in which men and women had highly affected mannerisms. Natasha, in *The Three Sisters,* a play set in 1901 in Russia, sometimes interrupts her native Russian to speak in French. As a peasant girl who has married into a higher-class family, she tries to imitate the sophisticated custom of using French phrases in conversation. However, she fails to realize that the custom is especially pretentious when adopted by middle- or lower-class persons—and poorly adopted at that. It is a great source of amusement for the other characters that Natasha abuses the custom, and the actors in this play must understand these circumstances to properly project the situation.

Historical Periods

Several periods in history have had a special impact on acting inasmuch as they developed distinctive styles. Accordingly, we can better understand these styles if we know the characteristics of each historical period—the political, social, economic, philosophical, and literary and dramatic movements and phenomena. The following periods are those most often encountered when performing in the theatre.

Greek Period
Roman Period
Commedia dell'Arte
Medieval and Tudor Periods
Elizabethan Period
Molière (Seventeenth-Century Neo-Classical Period)
English Restoration and the Eighteenth Century
Napoleonic or Empire Period
Romantic Period
Victorian and Edwardian Periods

Greek Period

Greek drama developed out of a ceremonial ritual honoring the spirit of the gods. Worshipers acted out simple dramas and assumed the roles of animals and natural forces to show their devotion, and a sacrifice was offered to symbolize the transfer of life from one individual to another. In the beginning, dramas were related by a chorus, but later a person would withdraw from the chorus and respond to the group. Then dialogue replaced narration. Later, as playwrights wrote plays that had many parts, actors began to train professionally. During the golden age of Greece, actors were highly trained professionals who were subsidized by the state, and were held in high regard and given special privileges.

Because Greek actors performed in large amphitheatres, actors had to have strong voices, and because the audience was sometimes separated from the stage by as much as a hundred yards, actors also had to be trained in special techniques of dance, mime, and gesture in order for their stage movements to be clear and meaningful. In classical fifth-century Greece, costumes were simple: soft buskin shoes and everyday chitons and himations (straight-line garments).

Costumes in the late Greek theatre were large, heavy, and colorful so that the audience could better see them. Also, because the dramatists wrote about kings and gods, the actors had to have a glorious stature. Leading actors wore a high headdress, wide, thick-soled shoes, body padding, ornamental robes, and masks, which were probably made of wood or cork. At times, the masks were not made to fit the face, but were placed

GREEK

GREEK

ROMAN

over the head to add to the impression of height. When emotions, such as happiness or sadness, were to be demonstrated, actors often changed their masks. Because masks served the same function as a megaphone in that they helped establish character and a larger-than-life quality, actors wore them for functional as well as decorative reasons.

Greek acting was highly stylized; that is, it was not "natural" or in conformity with the manners of everyday life. Audiences did not expect to see minor or highly personalized expressions of human desires; indeed, they were not interested in viewing the common experiences of the ordinary man. They came to the theatre to see heroes perform great and terrible deeds. This highly exaggerated acting style reinforced the belief in a universe of gods who participated in the lives of heroes and kings. At the same time, the style of acting was such that it carefully controlled the audience's involvement in emotional experience. According to Aristotle, an audience should feel "pity and fear" for the hero and then reach a "catharsis," that is, a "cleansing" of those emotions.

Thus, in the Greek ideal, emotion was artistically displayed on stage. Larger-than-life characters, wide, sweeping gestures, disproportioned bodies, and elaborate masks allowed the actor to maintain "psychic distance" from the audience and have better control of the emotional experience.

Roman Period

Acting styles in the Roman period modified the style of the late Greek or Hellenistic era. Roman tragedy, such as

ROMAN

the plays of Seneca, were never performed on stage. Instead, Roman drama focused on comedy, and particularly on the plays of Plautus and Terence. The comic style used in these plays did not require a range of complex emotions; the key emphasis was on clever timing and comic business. The plays focused on fighting, dancing, drinking, and flirtatious love scenes performed in street locales. Therefore, physical dexterity was essential, and costumes were again simplified, as in fifth-century Greece. Singing and dancing were utilized throughout the plays, as well as a less declamatory style of speech than was used by the Greeks.

Commedia dell'Arte

"Commedia," which used a loosely structured plot or outline and improvised dialogue, was a popular form of theatre during the Italian Renaissance. The plots and characters were taken from the plays written during the Roman period, and the themes usually concerned love and intrigue. Actors wore masks and costumes that were traditionally unique for their particular characters, such as a black robe and floppy hat for the scholar or a costume of brightly colored patchwork for the clown. Dialogue consisted of topical jokes and various "set" speeches for love scenes or quarrels. There were also juggling, ballet, and musical interludes.

**MIDDLE AGES
1200**

**COMMEDIA
DELL'ARTE**

Medieval and Tudor Periods

After the invasion of the Roman Empire by the barbarians, western Europe adhered to a very rigid social, economic, and religious system known as feudalism. Life held many hardships for the lowly serfs, who worked long hours on the manors. On the other hand, nobles had relatively pleasant lives, except when they fought their wars. Under feudalism, everyone paid homage to a king, who in turn was responsible to the church. During the medieval period, public theatres were closed, and commoners and nobles alike were enter-

LATE MIDDLE
AGES 1400

tained by bands of strolling players who were by profession, acrobats, jugglers, minstrels, and puppet masters. Then, in the eleventh or twelfth century, the church revived the dramatic dialogue that centered around the celebration of the Mass.

Church drama during the early Middle Ages was confined to simple situations, usually depicting scenes from the life of Christ. These were called "mystery" or "miracle" plays—though "miracle" usually referred to plays about saints, while "mystery" was more properly applicable to plays involving Christ. Townspeople, who performed in these plays, wore the clothes of the day —unadorned, long, loose robes for the lower classes and ornate, flowing robes or form-fitted, knee length tunics for the upper classes. Servants and noblemen portrayed themselves when they did not play the roles of Christ or members of the Holy Family. Later, in the fifteenth and sixteenth centuries, morality plays developed. Because these plays were concerned with virtues and vices, actors portrayed "qualities," such as goodness, hope, chastity, jealousy, anger, and greed to illustrate the theme of good versus evil.

During the Tudor period, fashions for the upper-class men and women began to change. Gentlemen wore padded breeches, so that their walk resembled a straddle, and wore hose to accentuate their legs. When sitting, men did not cross their legs, and when they stood they posed in what is known in ballet as the third position, with one foot slightly forward and turned out. Because men enjoyed wearing elaborate clothes, they gestured frequently to dramatize their finery. For example, if a man were wearing an elegant jeweled collar, he would put his hand to the collar and let it rest there, or if he wore a large ring, he might rest his hand across his chest and spread his fingers to display the jewels. The dress of upper-class ladies during the Tudor period stressed a form-fitting line. Waists were pinched by a corset and skirts were full and heavy. Although they found it difficult to sit and walk because of their tight and cumbersome clothes, they had to give the appearance of "floating through space."

It was a custom of the period for men to greet one another with both arms extended and to grasp one another simultaneously above the elbows or at the wrists. Women kissed each other when they met. Men and women held hands at informal gatherings; and when royalty was present, the gentleman's hand was extended forward at the shoulder, palm down, and the lady placed her fingertips on the back of his wrist.

Bows were another formal custom of the nobility. A nobleman removed his hat (usually before a king, lord, lady, or in church) and held it to his hip, or extended it behind him, took a step backward with one foot, bent halfway with both knees, and then straightened up. If he was not wearing a hat, he bowed and extended both arms behind him. An alternate bow was executed by holding one's hat on the hip or side, lunging forward with the right foot, and bending both knees. When a soldier came before a king, he knelt on one knee. Ladies curtsied by holding the skirt slightly out and bending both knees to a depth that accorded to the rank of the person being honored.

TUDOR PERIOD

ELIZABETHAN PERIOD

Elizabethan Period

Because his plays dominated the theatre during the last decade of the sixteenth century and the first decade of the seventeenth century, we usually associate the Elizabethan period with William Shakespeare. Shakespeare wrote during the Renaissance, when man was considered to be intelligent, free, resourceful, and the center of the universe, and his plays reflected this spirit. His heroes, who were larger than life, performed great and terrible deeds, suffered for their misdeeds, loved heroically, and fought valiantly. However, audiences could identify with the people in Shakespeare's dramas because they were every bit as sensitive and funloving as the characters who populated the Elizabethan plays.

Audiences during Shakespeare's time were composed of all kinds of people; seamen, apprentices, workers, middle-class merchants, wealthy landowners, and royalty. During performances, the audience drank, ate, smoked, and talked aloud. They enjoyed historical dramas, as well as comedies, tragedies, and romances, and did not mind that Shakespeare borrowed plots from history or folklore. Audiences focused on the various levels of characters, on the jokes and puns, the dialogue and rhetoric, and every other aspect.

In English classes you have studied some of the plays of Shakespeare, and you know that he usually wrote in blank verse or unrhymed iambic pentameter, which is very different from everyday speech. Shakespeare made every word convey a precise meaning or emotion, and every pause or repetition is planned for a predetermined dramatic situation.

Therefore, the lines should be delivered with exceptionally clear diction and with more or less perfunctory attention to movement and mannerisms. Inasmuch as the "style" of Shakespeare's characters is so strongly expressed or indicated in their speech, actors who play Shakespearean roles should develop their characters primarily from the study of plot and dialogue and, again, with appropriate emphasis on understanding human nature and behavior.

Molière

Molière's plays are notable for their exciting characters, comic situations, and brilliant language. Complicated and intricate, they require careful interpretation of the playwright's intent before the appropriate styles of acting can be determined.

Molière, who was an actor in the provinces of France during the period 1645 to 1658, was a member of a troupe of actors who performed in the tradition of the commedia dell'arte players. When he returned to Paris, in 1658 he began to write plays that ridiculed society and develop characters that corresponded to the types portrayed in the commedia. Molière ridiculed the aristocracy's extravagance and hypocrisy with corrective humor, laughing at his fellow countrymen in order to point out their foolish behavior and false values.

It is important that the actors in his plays take their roles seriously, for it is the serious demeanor of the characters that makes audiences laugh. True to the commedia dell'arte style of acting, actors must also use the body to help create interpretations of character. For example, a very erect posture or an expression

MOLIERE

of earnestness can make a character appear ridiculous in certain situations. Moreover, Molière wanted his actors to pay close attention to details of costume and custom. (Gentlemen wore wigs and perfume, carried lace hankerchiefs, and bowed frequently. Ladies carried fans, curtsied, moved with grace and ease, flirted, and toyed with men's affections.) All of Molière's characters should be played with zest and enthusiasm for life, for the action and dialogue move rapidly. Wit, intelligence, and sophistication are the trademarks of Molière's comedies.

Restoration and the Eighteenth Century

The term "Restoration" refers to the period after 1660, when Charles II was returned to the English throne and, after eighteen years of civil war and Puritan rule, the theatres were reopened to the public. As a reaction to the Puritan regime, the people enjoyed gaudy, naughty, and sophisticated dramas by such playwrights as Dryden, Etherege, Wycherley, Farquhar, and Congreve. Plays were concerned with the manners and affectations of the royal court and the upper classes. They were intellectual, stylish, sometimes cynical and sarcastic, and had inconsequential plots and characters modeled after those of Molière and the commedia dell'arte. For example, Restoration plays usually had one or two pairs of lovers, love scenes, trickery and deception, a fop or dandy, and a learned man. Playwrights did not attempt to conceal the hypocrisy, triviality, and immorality of the aristocracy.

It is good experience for young actors to learn some of the acting tech-niques appropriate for Restoration plays. One of the most important skills for acting in these so-called high comedies (comedies of manners) is making every movement and action precise, light, gay, and decorative. Pace is also very important. Because the play should move with the precision of a minuet, characters are usually devoid of a complex inner life. Although the playwrights saw the upper classes as spineless and artificial, at the same time they were utterly delightful because of their zest for life and fun.

To meet requirements of a Restoration play an actor must use bodily expressions of grace and personal attraction. The voice should be precise and bold to emphasize the playwright's wit, sophistication, and discipline. In addition, the actor might consider assuming an attitude of detachment for his or her character because this kind of comedy calls for little or no emotional identification on the part of the performer or the audience. At times, high comedy requires a detachment from the character in order to comment on the nature of that character. Only at rare moments need an actor identify with his or her character.

Restoration comedy also calls for moments of close audience-actor relationship. Audiences appreciate an intimacy with the actor, which allows both the actor and the audience to remain objective about the action. Such objectivity usually increases the willingness to laugh. Moreover, actors in Restoration plays often spoke directly to the audience in a confidential aside or candid remark, and thus audiences and actors can enjoy sharing a joke, as well as the characters' eccentricities. Laughter in these comedies usually results from a character's distortion of his or her personality, and indeed we always laugh at the exaggeration of a particular facet of a human being, such as being miserly or overly indulgent in matters of love and sex.

Dress during the Restoration period was ornate and decorative. Men wore square-cut coats that reached to the knees, wide and stiff cuffs with lace that reached to the knuckles, and lace shirts and collars. Breeches that broke below the knees, an ornate garter on one leg, red high-heeled shoes with buckles, large wigs with long curls, and a large broad-brimmed plumed hat completed the outfit. Accessories consisted of large fur muffs that hung at the belt, watches around the neck, canes, and small patches on the face in the shape of stars, triangles, or half-moons. Women wore wide, bell-shaped skirts, exposed necklines, high-heeled shoes, and hooded cloaks. They also wore heavy jewelry and black facial patches and carried a parasol, a sweets box, and a fan.

Manners, as well as dress, were formal. Married ladies and gentlemen greeted each other with a bow and a curtsy. A gentleman frequently kissed a lady's hand, and a lady walked beside a gentleman with her arm resting on his sleeve. Servants bowed when entering and leaving a room.

In high-heeled shoes, men had to walk with an erect posture and slow, deliberate steps. Contrary to popular conceptions, men were not always considered effeminate—in contrast to the fops of the time. Most men were very masculine and self-confident; women were ex-

tremely feminine and graceful, and walked as though moving on silk or gauze. To display their fine clothes, men posed when speaking (fops posed to an extreme), resting their weight on the back foot and placing the forward foot to the side. Hands were held high to show the lace cuffs and personal objects were handled with flourishes—handkerchiefs were waved and fans were fluttered almost constantly.

Snuff, taken to attract attention, was a matter of great ceremony. The snuff box was taken from the waistcoat pocket, tapped at the top to make the particles fall to the bottom. A pinch was taken with the thumb and second finger and either applied to the nose and inhaled, or placed on the back of the hand and sniffed. Then the cuffs were shaken to remove any clinging particles.

Bows were modified during the Restoration period. A lady simply curtsied and fluttered her fan. A gentleman stepped back, bent one knee, and placed his right hand over his heart, or placed his hand at his heart before the bow and brought it down before the lady with the palm open as he bowed. Or he would remove his hat and sweep it behind him on the right side. After bowing, he straightened up and brought his front foot back beside his rear foot. An informal bow, the "en passant," was used when passing one another outdoors. As they approached, they turned slightly to each other and bowed from the waist, sweeping one foot in an arc around the other as they continued walking.

Restoration style, manners, and customs dominated the first half of the eighteenth century with only minor modifications. The succeeding emphasis on

EIGHTEENTH CENTURY

morality and sentiment, along with the rise of the middle class, resulted in simpler and less ornate clothing and a more natural acting style, as advocated by David Garrick in England and Voltaire in France.

Napoleonic (or Empire) Period

The late eighteenth and early nineteenth centuries were characterized by great social upheavals and wars in Europe and the United States. America became a new nation by revolting against England; Russia, in effect, repulsed the attack of Napoleon, who was finally defeated at Waterloo in 1815. Theatre activity was slack during these troublesome times, but revivals of eighteenth-century plays were produced from time to time. The style of acting and costuming marked a transition from the complex, decorative, and declamatory work of the early eighteenth century. Costuming was simpler, but acting styles were moving toward the expansive and exciting era known as the romantic period, although speech and movement were still somewhat simpler or more natural.

Romantic Period

The romantic period, which flourished from approximately 1800 to 1850, was characterized by emotionalism rather than reason and by social unrest, creativity, individualism, freedom, and emphasis upon the basic rights of men. Men identified with the intangible and believed in a natural relationship with God, the sea, mountains, and the physical world in general. This was the period of the poets Blake, Wordsworth, Byron, Shelley, Keats, and Coleridge. In the theatre, such playwrights as Goethe and Schiller led the romantic movement.

Costumes were well tailored and richly detailed. Dresses were full length, heavy, and colorful; men's suits had the rather modern look of full-length trousers, handsome coats, and matching accessories. The acting style required skill in movement, dance, song, and pantomime. Presentations were characterized by flourishes in movement—large sweeping gestures and action. Speech was similarly loud, sweeping, and grand —once again in a highly declamatory manner.

NAPOLEONIC
PERIOD 1800

ROMANTIC PERIOD 1830

Victorian and Edwardian Periods

During the Victorian era, which is noted principally for its emphasis on morality and goodness, the melodrama developed as a form of theatre entertainment, depicting the virtues of goodness and the vices of evil. The characters in the melodrama consisted of the hero, the helpless heroine, and the villain. Costumes were not extravagant, although there was an emphasis on colorful sport clothes. In Victorian society, men played a very masculine role and were conscious of exemplifying "good breeding." They moved with assertiveness and ease.

It was the custom during this period to bow and curtsy when addressing one another, but by 1840 handshaking was common for men and ladies. Servants curtsied and bowed when announcing callers. Later, gentlemen bowed in the third ballet position, with one hand on the heart. When full skirts were in fashion, ladies curtsied in a formal stage bow, but the crinoline period ushered in a new kind of curtsy: bending of the right knee, followed by a slight bend backwards from the waist. A lady could perform this curtsy as long as her skirt was wide enough, and when her skirt was too narrow, she lifted it at the sides, took a step backward, and shifted her weight to her rear foot—always making certain that her ankles were covered.

Modern and Contemporary Periods

Toward the end of the nineteenth century, melodrama and the Victorian influence gave way to realism. Prior to this, the theatre was highly romantic in nature, its language was poetic, and realistic settings were not important. The realistic movement ushered in everyday dialogue, detailed stage directions and authentic settings, complex and psychological characterizations, and the common man.

Realistic Period

The principal exponent of realistic acting was Andre Antoine, a former clerk in a gas company who organized a free theatre in Paris. The main objective of Antoine's theatre, Le Théâtre Libre (The Free Theatre), was to produce plays that dealt with everyday subjects. He worked toward creating realism in stagecraft and reproducing every detail in an environment so that he almost literally brought the outside world into his theatre. His actors spoke the language of the common people and moved naturally and believably.

In the 1880s, realism began to spread throughout Europe from Paris, and to such countries as Russia, Ireland, and America during the early decades of the twentieth century. The contribution of Stanislavski and his method of realistic acting (discussed earlier in this text) to the realistic theatre was enormous in terms of both acting and stagecraft. Fortunately, much has been written about the man and his works, so that we can study this most important period in the modern theatre in depth. Indeed, in our three-year developmental acting program we have been primarily concerned with techniques for acting in the realistic theatre.

Realistic playwrights, such as Ibsen, Chekhov, Shaw, and O'Neill, wrote many plays, which call for an acting technique that probes the hidden depths of character and the values of society. Still, characters in realistic plays resemble ordinary people, who speak and act with simplicity. Thus, an audience can identify with these characters; that is, the audience can recognize aspects of themselves or people they know as they view the stage characters—some of the truths of daily living. Realistic actors, therefore, do not have to focus their acting on personal magnetism or on a beautiful, trained voice. The realistic actor concerns him or herself with acquiring the physical, vocal, emotional, and mental tools necessary for believable character creation.

Expressionism

Early in the twentieth century, certain artists revolted against the strong movement of realism in the theatre. Highly symbolic and poetic dramas were written by such playwrights as Maurice Maeterlinck. Finally, the Scandinavian playwright August Strindberg and the German playwright George Kaiser developed an exciting new form of drama called expressionism as a reaction against the industrial revolution and the theatre's undue emphasis on realism. The expressionists believed that man is becoming a machine, or a mere cog in a machine, and therefore, their plays reveal man in a dehumanized condition. Man performs as a robot, having lost all human identification; thus this acting style requires unique training in performing mechanically. This unusual approach to acting contributed to the later acting styles of the twentieth century, particularly the "absurd" and epic styles. The absurd and the epic styles combined expressionism with realism

and Oriental dramatic influences to form the so-called new drama.

Theatre of the Absurd or Absurd Drama

Something quite unique has happened in theatres over the past two decades, not just in America but in the theatres of every major western country. A new form of dramatic literature has appeared. No specific date marks the beginning of this new form; however, theatre historians will probably date the movement as appearing in France during the middle of the twentieth century. According to Charles Marowitz,

it . . . originated . . . with Irishman Beckett, the Rumanian Ionesco, and the Frenchman Genet. It found its first disciples in England in writers such as Harold Pinter and N. F. Simpson, and reached America in the words of Edward Albee, Arthur Kopit, and Jack Gelber. . . . It is a theatre devoted to exploration into our secret selves . . . its frame of reference is held together—not by our institutions, ideologies or class—but by our fears, our needs, our profoundest (untaught) beliefs. This new drama does not respect the traditional literary values. It rearranges, juxtaposes and sometimes forsakes conventional language. . . . In the new drama, language has become as functional as any other dramatic element.

Playwrights such as Barbara Garson, Megan Terry, and Jean Claude Van Itallie are depicting the political and social scene in the United States today in plays that tend to be a direct assault on the sensibilities of the audience. They seem to imply that the audience should think about our political and social problems and take action to correct the problems. Such groups as Julian Beck's Living Theatre and Circle-in-the-Square are attempting to produce domestic as well as foreign classics with a style that stresses free association and creative improvisation.

It can be readily seen that the style of acting in these plays demands both extraordinary freedom and carefully controlled techniques. Although the latter demand holds true for all acting, the new drama is generally construed by modern writers and directors as demanding extraordinary discipline and training in *all* acting methods to make these plays effective. Because the actor often is not supported by a story line or coherent dialogue, he or she must give meaning to the performance almost entirely on the basis of his or her own experiences and intellect. Often, a theatrical event is sparked by an idea or a character or a situation, and sometimes plays are created from various sensual impulses, with no elaborate plans for the actor. Often, these plays are not even completed.

To act in the new drama, according to Joseph Chaikin, director of the Open Theatre in New York, most actors should have extensive training in the so-called method or inspirational techniques as well as in the more traditional techniques, such as role analysis and other intellectual approaches (including the establishment of objective, obstacles, and like matter). Actors in new drama can analyze a text from the standpoint of both logic and emotion (which may be devoid of traditional logic, as is illustrated by sentences that do not connect meaningfully and seem to represent isolated feelings or pieces of information). Method training enables an actor to

probe the process of introspection, which allows him or her free use of personal resources in portraying a character. Traditional acting techniques teach an actor the disciplines of concentration, imagination, and observation, and help give strength and clarity to a role. Thus, the key to acting in the new drama is understanding and a balanced achievement of both the subjective and the objective approaches to the plays.

The primary emphasis in the experimental theatre of the new drama is on the performance of a variety of exercises in a troupe of actors, as opposed to individual work in characterization. Sessions usually begin with a "warm-up" exercise in which actors try to establish a common bond by mutual reflection upon their personal lives and problems, and further exploration may provide concepts or situations that can be worked into acting exercises. Most of the exercises deemphasize language per se and concentrate on communion through sounds (laughter and crying) and movements. Often, there is a choreographer who suggests a movement or rhythm that will express physical freedom. As an illustration, a group of actors may act out a bus ride, using very little language and concentrating more on expressions and movement.

If language is used in these exercises, the actors usually select sounds rather than words—for example, the sounds of people eating around a boarding-house table. The type of language or sounds depends on the goals and the themes of the improvisation. However, whatever the exercise, actors try to concentrate on what is *not* verbally expressed in the situation rather than on what *is* said. For example, a person could be drinking a glass of water while nervously wondering how to help his or her neighbor who is in debt, so that his or her mental concern will begin to reflect itself in the way he or she drinks the water. This can be accomplished by using "feeling" (the inspirational method) *and* technique (intellectual concentration and controlled actions).

Other exercises may pertain to the external world of reality, such as an exploration of advertising, which molds the image of the "American personality." The exercises are often satiric, thereby teaching actors to use the stage for social commentary, since most of the new-drama plays make observations about the social and political order in society. Sometimes the characters who are portrayed in these exercises are not recognizable as everyday people but appear as mental states or things, such as "American sloth" or a rubber ball. These kinds of exercises are excellent preparation for acting in plays by Beckett, Ionesco, Genet, and Van Itallie, who generally depict their characters as extensions of real-life people.

This experimental theatre is primarily interested in material that pertains to the mystery and illusion of life in the mid-twentieth century rather than that which pertains to realistic human behavior with its varied motivations. An actor in the new drama does not specifically create a set character from a didactic script and determine the form of his or her life; the character develops in any direction the actor's feelings and intellect indicate, often deviates completely from the script, which is used only as the actor's "springboard." This freedom and experimentation

arises out of the trust of fellow actors who are dedicated to the same goals, unafraid that failure will bring reprisals. Freedom, then, is the key to creative acting in the new drama—the kind of freedom that is learned from intensive introspection by method actors who can control their art with a sufficient balance of traditional acting techniques.

Although the acting that is associated with new drama appears to be very unstructured in its approach and contrary to what is learned by students at the beginners' levels, the basis for such freedom and experimentation is intensive study in the structured techniques of *realistic* acting. You should have complete control of the methods of self-discovery, character analysis, and body and voice flexibility before you begin to relate to the experimental theatre of the new drama.

Bertolt Brecht

("Theatre for Learning") An examination of modern theatre is not complete without a discussion of Bertolt Brecht (1898–1956), who more than any other modern playwright or producer was concerned with social action. Brecht called his theatre "epic," and he sought to bring about a change in the audience-actor relationship. His theories came to fruition in East Berlin in the 1940s and 1950s in Erwin Piscator's theatre, The Berliner Ensemble.

Brecht observed that for realistic plays the audience sat passively in a

The actor's own being must, at times, coincide with the emotions of the character.

theatre and viewed the events on stage as unchangeable or stable; therefore, he used the technique of portraying historical events on stage as though they were totally removed from present-day events. In doing this, Brecht wanted his audience to see the social ills of the past and to realize that, had the viewers lived in those times, corrective action could have been taken. Then, as the audience examines present-day society, it can see that things have changed and that it is possible to accomplish social reform. Perhaps Brecht's theory of theatre was influenced primarily by his political philosophy; he was a Marxist and a propagandist, as well as a poet. He believed that the function of the theatre is to instruct, and not with the emotions but with the intellect. Audiences, he held, should respond to the social, economic, political, and moral conditions of society.

To increase the responsiveness of the audience to social change, Brecht also advocated a concept known as *alienation*, which means "to make strange." Brecht wanted his audiences to be aware of the make-believe nature of the events on stage so that they could "see through" the theatrics and could concentrate on the conditions of society. The audience is then free to watch critically and thoughtfully.

Brecht called his theatre epic because he felt that the plays resembled epic poems rather than realistic dramas. His plays are a combination of dialogue and narration in which time is bridged and scenes may be either dramatized or narrated.

Brecht was influenced by the German director Erwin Piscator in Berlin in the 1920s. Piscator, an innovator in stagecraft, used many special devices to help dramatize events: treadmills, projections, scenic fragments, giant caricatures, and many other devices as comments on the action on stage. Brecht, similarly, did not want to be realistic in his staging; he wanted to comment on society and to arouse the audience to become involved outside the theatre. He wanted audiences to carry the messages of his plays to the people at large.

Antonin Artaud

("Total Theatre") Perhaps the most influential of all theatre directors was Antonin Artaud (1896–1948). Although his theatre was based in France, it was also based primarily on the Oriental concept of drama—nonverbal, magical, and musical, and oriented to the senses. Artaud called his theatre the "theatre of cruelty" because he assaulted the audience's self-control. In an attempt to make his viewers turn inward and discover the mysterious part of their existence, he used a barrage of visual and aural experiences as an expression of total artistry. The verbal text was a "minimum structure." To Artaud, sensual experiences were the key to opening a man's inner self so that he could better communicate with himself and society.

Jerzy Grotowski and the Polish Laboratory Theatre

Today's most influential director-pro-ducer is Jerzy Grotowski, director of the Polish Laboratory Theatre, who has written and spoken extensively about his theatre and his technique of teaching acting. Although he was influenced by Stanislavski, Grotowski's solutions to acting problems (specifically, the problem of believability) are different from those of the Stanislavski method. In effect, Grotowski combines a variety of western and Oriental acting techniques that require many years of exhaustive mental, physical, and emotional training. He feels that the more the actor becomes involved with understanding and controlling himself, the more successful he or she will be in artistic expressiveness. This will lead to complete body and emotional control, and total self-discipline, on stage.

The involvement of the audience will be heightened by concern for a more spiritualized confrontation with the actors. Through a kinetic relationship, audiences will participate in the agonies and torments of existence, in the suffering of all human beings. Grotowski calls his theatre "holy" because of its concern for self-knowledge, self-sacrifice, and a total commitment to human existence. The basis for the psychic relationship between audience and actor is sympathy, warmth, and understanding. Because every human is engaged in acquiring self-knowledge, a strong bond is created when the audience sees this process at work in an actor's performance.

The actor's primary goal, then, is to free himself from all associations and expressions that lead to a lack of discipline and that obstruct self-knowledge. All obstacles to attaining "holiness" must be eliminated through rigorous and disciplined training.

REHEARSAL TIME

Activity

1. Take a play from one of both the historical and contemporary periods and compare them on the different aspects of an actual play analysis. For instance, what are the differences in the types of characters and the different ways the actor would have to approach studying them? What is different about the language in each of the plays? How does this affect the actor? What about the set-tings? Customs? Clothes? Family relationships? Political relationships? Views on religion, sex, marriage, families? What about racial implications? In other words, compare the plays in every facet that would be important to an actor when researching the background for a play. Record these findings in your theatrical notebook. Be prepared to support your views and discuss your findings with the rest of your acting group.

CURTAIN

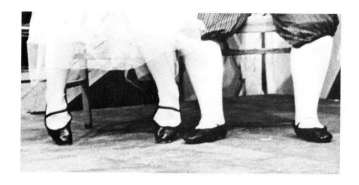

When studying acting at the advanced level, the actor must consider the matter of style, which is an approach to a play through the study of a particular period. Research should be conducted into the appropriate costumes, manners, customs and dialects. However, actors must be careful to recognize that the historical period of a play is not always an automatic indication of the style of acting required for a play. Specifically, style as an external detail should be considered. It should also be performed in a manner appropriate to the character.

Scene Four

FUTURE FRONTIERS

Many new actors wish to pursue the study of drama beyond the amateur level. Some of the questions asked by these new actors are; How can someone become a teacher of acting? How does one become a professional actor or director? Is it difficult to get a job in summer stock? How does someone get involved in community theatre? What if someone simply wants to be a consumer of drama? Hopefully, these questions will begin to be answered in this last section of the book.

University and Community Theatre

Nearly every university and college in the United States offers a program in theatre arts. Some universities specialize in various facets of theatre, such as acting, the technical aspects of theatre, costuming, or scenery design. Most programs however, offer general theatre studies in which students can major or minor in drama and obtain a well-rounded theatre education.

If becoming a teacher of drama is important, the beginning actor should pursue studies on the university level. Those performers who are looking toward a professional theatre career should also consider university theatre for basic background. Although the university student is required to take a variety of courses in the humanities and sciences at the university level, some professionals feel that a general education broadens the interests and intellectual ability of the actor. In addition, acting students are able to gain valuable experience by participation in college productions. By assuming a variety of responsibilities, whether as technicians, actors, costumers, designers, directors, or playwrights, the beginning actors get to view the theatre from all angles. Some universities actually gear their courses toward careers in the professional theatre.

Many new actors may be looking for a career position as a teacher in educational theatre. This may be at the primary level, where creative drama enhances the growth of young children. Or it may be at the secondary level, where older children are able to express themselves in a variety of theatre activities both in and out of the school. Teaching drama is an extremely rewarding profession, both in the classroom and in the theatre. Educational theatre provides a stability and continuity of occupation that is unique in the world of theatre. In order to become a teacher of drama, the actor must go to college for at least a bachelor's degree. To teach at the college level, a master's degree and probably a doctorate degree are required.

The best way to choose a college or university that will provide the most beneficial curriculum is to consult college catalogues and the theatre representatives from prospective schools. This procedure affords the student a chance to compare different programs and to choose the one most suitable. Another resource might be the directory of the American Theatre Association. This gives a fairly complete listing of schools that offer degrees in theatre.

When funds are lacking to attend a good theatre arts program, but the will for a career in theatre is nevertheless present, the actor may have to attend a college or university that does not have an extensive program in theatre. Remember, however, that any theatre program offers experience that will prove beneficial in later years. On the other hand, part-time jobs and scholarships might provide the needed financial assistance that will enable you to go to a good school.

One of the realities of college life that theatre students have to accept is

that higher education is based on a competitive grading system, which suspends students who do not maintain a certain grade point average. Drama students, of course, have a particularly difficult time maintaining good grades because of the constant demand on their time by both the theatre department and the university. For example, an acting or directing class requires that time be spent out of class rehearsing scenes. Students who take technical theatre courses must also spend many hours in rehearsal with university theatre productions to gain experience with scenery, lighting, costuming, and sound effects. Drama students, therefore, must budget their time very carefully and study all their courses. Indeed, most of their spare time must be devoted to study and practice.

Community theatre draws on even its youngest members.

In college and professional life, the theatre demands nearly all the actor's time and devotion, and it is very difficult to forego the normal social functions because of rehearsals or the like. However, the actor should be willing to sacrifice some social pleasures for theatre activities. The theatre can be an all-encompassing vocation that requires tremendous commitment from the university student. The actor must learn a rigorous craft that takes constant on-the-job experience. Proficiency comes only through dedication.

Many students will select careers and employment in fields other than drama. Yet, with age, comes an eagerness to remain close to the theatre, to participate in its activities. Those who reside in cities that sponsor a community theatre will have an opportunity to utilize their skills and knowledge about the theatre. They may also help others achieve a quality of performance.

Teamwork is at the center of community theatre. Plays are selected by the director, reading committees, or the entire theatre group. After the decision is made to produce a specific play, the publicity committee announces tryouts to the general public. If plays are precast, the community soon feels the so-called "community theatre" is just another dramatic club and the purpose of opening theatre to the public is defeated. Precasting should be avoided. Once the play is cast, rehearsals begin immediately and continue for six to eight weeks. While the play is in rehearsal, another play can be decided upon and cast from the community. If only two or three plays are to be produced in a season, casting for the next production can be postponed until the first production is closed. However, community theatre should be a continuous process in order to maintain the importance in the community and among the theatre members. Continuity increases the public's acceptance of the theatre and its place in civic life.

Community theatre offers a tremendous challenge to drama students who attend high school or college. Participating in community theatre is often a means by which the actor can increase dramatic experience. If the actor has many talents to offer the theatre, its members will be helped by sharing this knowledge. The experiences brought to the theatre from the high school or college help to increase the overall general standards.

Community theatre attracts a wide variety of talented people and people who are interested in the theatre. Most of them are motivated to participate because of their desire to perpetuate the so-called "living theatre." Those who join the group have a variety of theatrical backgrounds—high school, college, summer stock, and professional—and some will be totally inexperienced. Often, men and women who work at local radio and television stations find stimulation through work in community theatres. At any rate, community theatre attracts great numbers of people, both as participants and as members of the audience, who are very interested in, or skilled and knowledgeable about theatre arts. This factor adds another dimension to community theatre, making it a real cultural asset rather than just an exercise in community cooperation.

Except for the director, the secretary, and possibly a designer and choreographer (all of whom are salaried), community theatre is completely noncommercial. All workers are volunteers and every member of the group has equal status. Nevertheless, everyone is expected to give maximum cooperation in every endeavor and to eschew egotism, pettiness, and jealous rivalries. Honesty and integrity are essential. Because no one is a member of Actor's Equity, union rules are not applicable. Each member is responsible for the workload assigned.

Acting as a profession can come at any age. Many have come to acting after sixty-five!

Summer Stock and Professional Theatre

Many actors and directors have gotten their starts in the theatre by working in summer stock companies. Summer stock refers to the semiprofessional or professional theatre companies that produce plays throughout the United States and other countries for an entire summer. They may also produce a repertory of plays, which is a sequence of plays done over several days, weeks or months. These theatres usually open in June and close at the end of August. Summer stock offers both amateur and professional actors a wide variety of experiences.

The salary of a summer stock company depends on many things. Apprentices usually receive little or no money. Their hours are long, their work is strenuous and exhausting, and their rewards are derived basically from the work itself. However, they are usually learning a craft and are receiving valuable experience working with professional directors, actors and technicians.

One of the characteristic features of summer stock is the super-intense atmosphere, which is rarely encountered in university and high school productions. The primary objective is to produce a play as fast as possible. Even if only one play is to be produced for the summer months, members of the company work at a frenzied pace to get it "on its feet." Lines are learned quickly; scenery is built on the spot; costumes are prepared

and ready in the first week; rehearsals are held every day and all day but for no more than a week.

If a company is producing plays in a repertory, the regular procedure is to rehearse one play during the day and produce another at night. Scenery and costumes are sometimes made in a single day and lines are learned in a matter of hours. Plays are not rehearsed over six weeks, or even one week, but often in a mere twenty-four hours.

If the actor is willing to accept the rigorous demands of summer stock, this theatre experience can be valuable for work in other kinds of professional theatre, such as New York theatre and year-round repertory companies.

Students who aspire to professional theatre careers will probably have a

most difficult and challenging future. Very few of them will achieve "big time" success. Competition is keen and sometimes fierce among the many thousands who want to establish professional theatre careers. Those who achieve success usually do so by capitalizing on unique opportunities.

Many may believe they will be the one exception, that they will be discovered quickly, having read about those who became famous in a short time. However, this percentage is very small. Most of the professionals have pursued their careers for many years. The theatre is full of actors, directors, technicians, and designers who have not achieved popularity, let alone stardom. Nevertheless, they are professionals who keep the wheels of theatre turning.

No matter where a professional career might lead, whether in the movie or TV industry, in New York, or in repertory theatre in other cities, there will be financial problems. Most actors find part-time jobs while attending classes or looking for permanent theatre employment. If admitted to a repertory company, the actor may find that the apprentice's wages are not sufficient on which to live. If attending classes during the day, the actor may be a waiter by night.

In trying to become established as a professional, the actor will have to develop perseverance and be willing to devote whatever time is required to increase theatre experience. Above all, an actor must keep a good morale and good physical condition. Only through self-confidence will an actor be able to survive the professional world. No aspiring actor can afford to lack self-confidence, not even those who are discovered early in their careers. A positive attitude will help maintain high standards and self-respect.

If an actor is both persistent and lucky, eventually there will be a chance to display talents and knowledge, the "break." A producer of director, for whatever reason, may suspect talent and give the actor a chance to "make good." A producer may give an aspiring director an opportunity to direct a play on Broadway, or a director may decide that a young actor can successfully play a difficult role. An established scene designer may have another commitment and thus provide an unknown the opportunity to design the setting for a play. Such opportunities are unpredictable. Often they come down to being in the right place at the right time and talking to the right person. There is no formula for getting a "break." This is one reason why anyone aspiring for a theatrical career may be in for heartbreak.

One way actors compete for employment is through auditions. When auditioning for a play, the actor reads from a script before a group of producers, directors, and writers. The actor is judged on a number of criteria known only to the panel. If the script is new, it must be read "cold." If the script is a revival, research can be done before the audition.

Auditioning for a play requires excellent reading qualities and an intuitive ability to analyze characters. If an actor is a poor reader, or cannot interpret a play quickly, additional acting lessons would be advisable for enhancement of these techniques.

Once chosen to work in the theatre, either on an apprenticeship or by a professional contract, the actor may want to obtain a theatrical agent, who is employed to assist the artist in gaining employment. An agent receives a percentage of the artist's gross income (usually 10 percent), and the artist generally provides the agent with a personal resumé and photographs. However, an agent does not necessarily solve an artist's employment problems. The agent may find potential jobs, but the artist must compete with others to get the position. In other words, the final success rests solely with the actor.

The Theatre Consumer

All of us will continue to be consumers of drama and the theories and exercises in this book have a dual purpose in helping everyone become a better, more aware, discriminating and satisfied theatre-goer. Additionally, all of the work done in acting will have a constructive influence on the personalities of the people that participate in it. Acting can aid in "bringing out" the best in us.

REHEARSAL TIME

The following is an exercise that can be used the rest of your active theatre life. It is a research activity to activate thoughts about future theatre careers and future thoughts about theatre in general and how you will relate to it.

Activity

1. As a group or as an individual, research different theatre programs in the various universities and try and have representatives from those universities visit your group. If there is a local community, university, or professional theatre nearby, go and see a play, and try to get permission to talk with the cast and crew members about their parts in the theatre world. Try to attend as many plays as possible and try out for local productions yourself. Review the notes you have made in your theatrical notebooks and take inventory of where you have come and possibly where you may be going.

CURTAIN

    This book has been directed primarily toward the new acting student who is interested in learning about acting in the theatre or in simply enjoying drama as a better educated consumer of the arts. Each section has tried to increase the beginning actor's skills and broaden the attitudes and understanding of the theatre world.

    Everyone will of course be a consumer of theatre. The question is how many will want to become producers of drama? In both instances, it is imperative that high artistic standards in the theatre are maintained and that theatre knowledge be shared so that more people will attend theatre productions with insight and enjoyment.

EPILOGUE

THE OTHER SIDE OF THE CURTAIN

The cast of a play are the stars of a performance that receive audience recognition. On the other side of the curtain is an entire team of stars who receive little public recognition for their long hours of artistic work. This cast consists of artists, designers, technicians, publicists, and crews that work diligently to make a performance possible. Each one of these crew heads and their teams is highlighted in the pages ahead and deserve a standing ovation.

Nonprofessional Theatre Organization Chart*

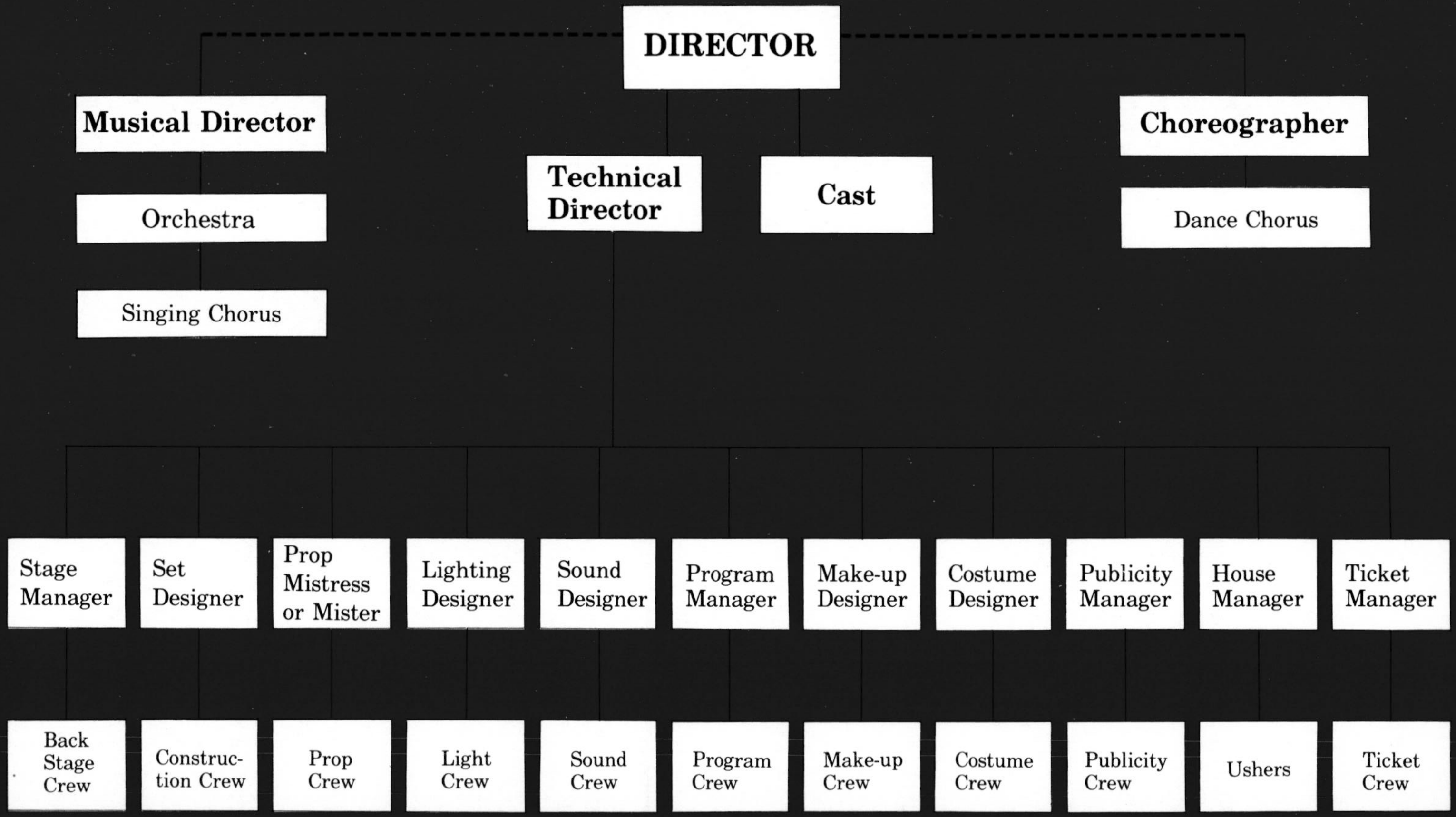

DIRECTOR

Musical Director

Orchestra

Singing Chorus

Technical Director

Cast

Choreographer

Dance Chorus

Stage Manager

Set Designer

Prop Mistress or Mister

Lighting Designer

Sound Designer

Program Manager

Make-up Designer

Costume Designer

Publicity Manager

House Manager

Ticket Manager

Back Stage Crew

Construction Crew

Prop Crew

Light Crew

Sound Crew

Program Crew

Make-up Crew

Costume Crew

Publicity Crew

Ushers

Ticket Crew

*Depending on the nature of the theatre groups, this organizational structure and the titles may vary somewhat.

Technical Director

In nonprofessional theatre, the technical director may coordinate all areas outside of the role of director, choreographer, and musical director. This function has direct contact with the director in planning, discussing, and implementing an integrated performance. The Nonprofessional Theatre Organization Chart illustrates the relationship of the crew head and the technical director.

Stage Manager

The stage manager is the *one person in control* backstage. It is the responsibility of the stage manager to double check with all backstage crew managers to make sure the performance is ready before the house manager opens the doors for the audience. Then, upon cue from the house manager, the stage manager gives the command to begin the performance. The stage manager is the BOSS of cast and crew backstage. The person in this role has the responsibility to oversee all backstage functions. The stage manager also helps solve those unexpected problems that happen during every performance. He or she usually selects the backstage crew from those who have worked the hardest on their crew functions. It is an honor to be selected as a member of the backstage crew.

Set Designer

The set designer is responsible for the design of all the scenery used in a production. The set designer works closely with the technical director and the director in planning the design and the movement of the scenery. In the case of a musical, the designer also works with the choreographer and musical director. This individual is in charge of overseeing the construction, painting, and installation of the scenery. In productions where there are massive complicated sets, the set designer may appoint a construction head to supervise the set construction crews. When selecting the paint colors for the set, the set designer works closely with the lighting designer to ensure the creation of the proper moods and feeling for the production. During actual construction, the set designer establishes a work schedule for the crew to construct the sets. This schedule must be coordinated with other rehearsals on stage. The set must be ready for the first technical rehearsal. The designer is also responsible for ordering all supplies, keeping accurate records of expenditures, checking all tools, supervising each clean-up after each construction work session, and supervising the "strike" after the show. These tasks are closely coordinated with the technical director.

Prop Mistress or Mister

The person that fills this area of responsibility works diligently to organize a team to manage the props. The play script must first be read with attention to details. Notation of the props required must be made. The prop crew must provide those necessary items that fit the need and the period of the production. Props must be provided early in the rehearsal stages of a production. Sometimes as actors work with the props during rehearsals, the director will request changes. One of the most difficult functions of the prop crew is to collect, repair, and store the props. Props have a way of getting lost. A seasoned prop mistress or mister will work closely with the crew on the entire organization system involved with props. Props should be kept and stored to develop a prop warehouse for additional productions.

Lighting Designer

The lighting designer creates the light plots, implements their installation, and oversees the operation of the lights during rehearsals and productions. The complexity of a production and the equipment available determine the difficulty of the lighting designer's duties. This person works closely with the director, set designer, and technical director. The lighting designer supervises a team who must clean, check, set, reset, and operate the lights. In some instances, additional lighting equipment

needs to be rented for a complex production. The effect created by the lighting team must be supportive of the feeling and the mood the director is trying to create.

Sound Designer

The sound designer has two main technical functions: sound effects and amplification. The director and the technical director work with the sound designer to determine the effect and the placement, or cue, for the effect. The use of amplification is dependent upon the production, the size of the theatre, and the philosophy of the director. The sound crew, who reports to the sound designer, sets, maintains, and operates all sound equipment. Since sound equipment is expensive, security of the equipment is paramount.

Program Manager

The manager of the program works with the technical director, publicity manager, ticket manager, and all other crew managers to collect the names of all those who have contributed to the production. A careful listing with numerous proofreadings is a sizable task for any one crew. If the program is used for advertising or fund raising, the program crew usually works closely with the publicity crew in coordinating their promotion. It is the responsibility of the program manager to present an accurate document. All the financial arrangements, such as printing costs and ad space sold, are also the responsibility of the program manager.

Make-Up Designer

Successful make-up involves a good working relationship between the make-up designer, the technical director, and the director. Basically, the make-up designer plans all the make-up for all the characters in the play. The feeling and mood of the play is one prime concern. The other major concern is the visability of the character's facial expression to the audience. In addition to creating make-up plots for each character, the make-up designer is responsible for ordering make-up, inventory and general clean-up. The members of the make-up crew are assigned certain characters to work with from the first make-up rehearsal. In the early stages of the make-up rehearsals, adjustments to the make-up need to be made if the design does not work well with the lights and costumes. Responsible crew members keep close watch on their make-up kits to prevent loss and waste.

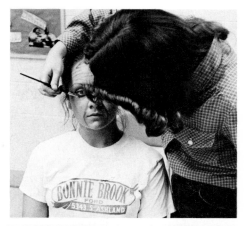

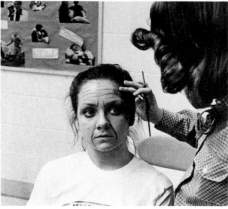

Costume Designer

The costume designer prepares costume designs for all characters in a production. The costume designer works with the director and the technical director regarding the specifics. The costume designer may elect to construct or rent costumes, depending on the production and the budget. In many instances, a combination of construction, borrowing, and renting is used. Some theatre groups have an expansive group of stock costumes from previous productions for use. The costume designer and crew are responsible for all fitting, cleaning, and storage of costumes during a production. If the crew does not pay attention to the smallest detail, the costumes and accessories have a way of getting lost during rehearsals and performances.

Publicity Manager

The publicity manager works closely with the director and the technical director to plan a total campaign for promotion of the production. Working with a crew, the publicity manager begins *before* tryouts, publicizing the tryout dates of the play. From the early point and through the rehearsal stages, the publicity manager plans a complete promotion schedule. No matter how much work and creativity are expended on a production, without an audience, no one will appreciate it. Depending on the production and the budget, the publicity manager must plan a campaign to draw audiences. More importantly, the campaign must reflect the mood of the production. The publicity manager and crew must be careful not to establish false expectations of an audience. The size of the house determines the success of the publicity manager and crew.

House Manager

The house manager works with the technical director, the stage manager, and the box office staff to coordinate the function. The start of each performance and audience control are the main duties. The ushers are the house crew. It is their duty to collect tickets, seat patrons, distribute programs, and handle special seating arrangements. Temperature control of the house is another important responsibility. In some instances, the house crew is obtained from those members who have worked on publicity and tickets. Individual theatre organization and number of available persons determines this area of staffing.

Ticket Manager

The ticket manager and crew work closely with the publicity manager. Ticket design, sales, and distribution of tickets to all cast and crew are the major responsibilities of the ticket manager. Distribution of complimentary tickets (when appropriate) to friends of the theatre is another duty. Accurate record–keeping and deposits of the monies from sales is a vital function for the ticket crew and managers. Box office sales prior to the production, and during the nights of the performance are handled by the manager and crew. Since large sums of money may be involved, responsibility is the key to success in every facet of the production.

STUDENT NOTEBOOK

The student notebook can be an invaluable aid to the student actor if kept consistently and diligently. It can act as a "yardstick" measure of where the actor has been, where the actor is now, and possibly where the actor should be going next. By writing the information, the actor can begin to solidify ideas and clarify thoughts by placing pen to paper.

It might be helpful to organize the notebook in this manner.

Of course this is not the only manner of organizing the theatrical notebook, but it has been used successfully by many students in the past. If another format is used, it should be consistent throughout the notebook so that comparisons can be made to show progression throughout the course. It should also try to cover somewhat the same information as this format.

DATE:

SUBJECT BEING DISCUSSED:

IMPORTANT VOCABULARY AND DEFINITIONS:

LECTURE NOTES:

LOG OF EXERCISES AND PERSONAL IMPRESSIONS:

INFORMATION LEARNED:

CRITICISMS AND IMPROVEMENTS:

INFORMATION FOR FUTURE PROJECTS OR HOMEWORK:

9/26 Stage Areas

VOCABULARY upstage, downstage, centerstage, rightstage, leftstage

EXERCISE We took turns walking through the different stage areas. It was easy until we had to make turns and walk with our backs to the audience. Then the right and left stage are reversed. The stage is divided up

Down Left	Down Center	Down Right
Center Left	Centerstage	Center Right
Up Left	Up Center	Up Right

Backstage

An actor has to be familiar with this terminology. This would be good test information!

HOMEWORK Read section on body positions. Explain them.

12/12 Emotion Study

VOCABULARY none

CLASS NOTES It is important that emotional scenes are played simply and shouldn't get overdramatic. Don't try to fake crying. Think of something sad.

EXERCISE Pick a character in a happy or sad situation. Decide what character is doing and why he or she is feeling that way. I chose a clown whose mother just died and who has to perform.

INFORMATION LEARNED These scenes are not easy. You have to keep a straight face for both comedy and tragedy.

CRITICISM AND IMPROVEMENT I am distracted by the audience. They make me laugh. I need more work on concentration.

HOMEWORK Read other emotional scenes. Be prepared to do a duet using another emotion. Play must be read by 12/19. Test Friday.

GLOSSARY

Absurd Drama A form of theatre in which language becomes the unconventional, and in which political and social problems are examined and presented to the audience in unconventional ways.

Adaptation A change on the spur of the moment due to unforeseen circumstances. Usually this is used in relation to improvisation.

Ad Lib To create action and dialogue without a prepared script. Acting on the spur of the moment.

Antagonist The person or force working against the protagonist in the play.

Antecedent Events Events preceding the opening of a play that have a bearing on the action within the play.

Antipathetic Forces working against the protagonist.

Articulation The clear and concise pronunciation of words and sounds.

Aside Lines that are said by a character, usually to the audience, outside of the action happening on stage.

Auditions Try-outs for positions in a play.

Beats A unit of rhythm within a particular section of a play or scene.

Blocking The decision-making process of directing action on stage.

Build To heighten the intensity of action within a scene or an entire play.

Burlesque Farce A broad exaggerated comedy.

Business Extra actions or pantomime used to add to a scene.

Casting The choosing of actors for particular roles in a play.

Center Stage The exact center on a conventional stage.

Chain Improvisation An improvisation in which characters move in and out of the scene, causing it to expand in depth and complication.

Character A person in a play.

Characterization Putting the particular facets of a character together to make a believeable person on stage.

Character Role A role in which the actor has to take on traits that differ from his or her own, producing the character desired.

Climax The highest or most exciting point in a play or scene.

Cold Reading The reading of a script, usually at an audition, without any prior knowledge of the material.

Comedy A play dealing with the humorous treatment of characters and situations.

Commedia Dell'Arte A type of play popular during the Italian Renaissance, which combined many art forms in the actual production of the play. Plays were usually taken from Roman classics.

Communication The exchange of ideas through speech or other forms of interchange.

Community Theatre Theatre produced by an independent group within a particular community to further the artistic goals of the community.

Concentration The ability to focus the mind and body toward a given goal. The most important ability of an actor.

Context Looking at a particular scene within the overall framework of a play. Could also be looking at particular characters or lines within the play.

Conventional Stage An acting area in which the audience is in front of the actors and some type of backdrop or wall is at the rear of the actors.

Costumes Clothing that is used to further the illusion of a particular character on the stage.

Costume Props Properties that are attached to or part of a particular character's clothing.

Crisis The highest point of conflict in a play or scene.

Cross To move from one area of the stage to another.

Cue A signal for an actor to speak or move on stage.

Dialogue A verbal interaction between two or more characters.

Diction The pronunciation of words.

Director The person in charge of bringing a production together from all sides: the acting, the technical, the publicity, etc. The person in charge of a production as a whole.

Discourse The formal combination of words into meaningful patterns.

Discovery The finding out of important information within a play that was previously unknown.

Dominant In a position of power. Could be either a person or an area.

Downstage The area of the stage closest to the audience.

Drama A literary composition to be performed on stage.

Dress Rehearsal The final rehearsal before opening night. This rehearsal is usually done in costume with all technical portions of the production added.

Drop The dropping of volume on the last word or words of a speech.

Elizabethan A period of English drama dominated by the plays of William Shakespeare and others of his style of writing.

Emotion Memory The replacement of an actor's feelings for a character's feelings. A technique used by Stanislavski.

Empathy The flowing of emotion from the actor to the audience and its return.

English Restoration Intellectual, stylish plays concerned with the affectations and manners of the royal court and upper class of England after 1660.

Environment The total setting and feeling in which a particular scene is played.

Epic A narrative play with a dignified style.

Expressionism A highly symbolic and poetic type of playwrighting, usually in revolt against realistic forms of drama.

Exposition Information discovered in the beginning of the play to set up for the action that is to follow.

Facial Expression Any ideas or emotions expressed through the use of the facial muscles.

Falling Action Action that occurs between the climax and the final curtain.

Fantasy A play dealing with unrealistic and fantastic characters. Childrens' plays are usually fantasies.

Flexibility The ability to use the voice in a wide range of volume, pitch, and rate.

Gestures Movements made with the hands and arms.

Greek Period A highly stylized type of drama originating in the worship of Greek gods.

Hand Props Any properties carried on stage by an actor.

Identification Taking experiences from the actor's life, and for motivation, relating them to a character.

Illusion Making the audience believe the actions on stage within the framework of the play.

Impromptu Performing without advance preparation.

Improvisation Performing without preparation, on the spur of the moment.

In Character When on stage, performing as a character and never becoming the actor, rather than the character, while performing.

Inflection The variation of the voice to produce certain feelings and emotions in words.

Intensity The use of vocal variation to produce a feeling of power and control in the voice.

Interaction The relating of two or more people on stage.

Interpret To analyze a piece of literature and perform it aloud for an audience.

Locales The geographical settings of scenes within a play.

Mannerisms Idiosyncrasies that make each person different, whether they be verbal, physical, or psychological. They prove very helpful in the creation of a character.

Medieval and Tudor A period in which religious and mystery plays were dominant. The style was formal and stilted, and the plays usually held a moral.

Melodrama A romantic play with extravagant emotions and usually a happy ending.

Method Acting A technique used by actors in which the actor tries to become the character in as many ways as possible. This facilitates a realistic performance.

Motivation The reason behind an action or line. Why something is done.

Mystery A play, usually from the medieval period, depicting the life of Christ.

Monologue A speech given by a single character, usually of dramatic nature.

Napoleonic or Empire A transitionary period in the eighteenth century, varying from extravagant styles of acting and costuming to simpler modes.

Nonverbal Communication Any communication that does not involve speech. This could include gestures, body language, facial expressions, etc.

Pace The rate and flow of action within a scene or a play.

Pantomime The telling of a story without the use of language. It consists of the use of the entire body and pantomime techniques.

Pause A lull or stop in action, dialogue, or verbal utterance.

Personal Props Properties on the actor's person such as eyeglasses, rings, etc.

Pick-up a Cue To be ready to perform an action or line immediately when the cue is given.

Pitch The high and low of a person's voice.

Play A form of writing, intended for live performance, consisting of characters and dialogue.

Playwright A writer of plays.

Plot The storyline behind a play.

Posture The physical way an actor holds his or her body. Good posture is important for proper projection on stage.

Precast To have people in mind for parts in a play before an audition is held. This is not a good practice because it forms a bias in both the director and the actors auditioning.

Project To increase the volume and quality of the voice so as to be heard clearly and concisely by all of the audience.

Pronunciation The particular way a word or phrase is to be said.

Props Anything moveable on stage that is not considered a part of the set or costuming.

Protagonist The main character in a play and who the play is written about. Usually, this is the hero or heroine.

Range The distance in pitch between an actor's highest and lowest tones.

Rate The speed with which something is done or said.

Rehearsal A period of time used to prepare a play for presentation to an audience.

Relaxation The ability to release tension from the body and still keep control for quick reactions.

Repertory Theatre A group of performers that produce plays in short periods of time and present them to the public.

Resolution The solution of the climax within a play. Usually comes during the falling action after the climax.

Resonance The ability of the sound to vibrate within the head. This gives a depth to the vocal quality of a performer.

Reversal A change of flow of the action within a play.

Roman Period A modification of the Greek style of acting, dominated by comedies.

Rhythm The variation of pace within an actor's voice.

Satire Plays in which vices or follies are held up to contempt.

Scene A small segment of a play, usually containing one central idea or line of action.

Script The written text of a play.

Selection Drawing attention to specific objects on stage to convey an idea through the object.

Set The physical backdrop for a play that is built on the stage.

Spectacle A production that uses an abundance of costuming, extra people, and extravagant sets to overwhelm the audience.

Speech Patterns The idiosyncrasies in a voice that make it individual and unique.

Stage Anywhere that actors and audience are combined to produce a performance.

Stage Props Items or objects that relate to the set.

Stimulus Anything that starts the thinking process or that awakens one of the senses. The motivation behind a reaction.

Straight Role A role in which the actor and the character are similar. The actor makes small changes to accommodate the differences in the part.

Style The manner in which a play was written and the period to which it relates.

Subordinate A character or position that is of less power than another character or position.

Substitution The use of one of the actor's experiences to relate to the experience of a character within a play.

Subtext The creation of character traits, and perhaps actions, not specifically outlined in the action of a play.

Summer Stock Plays presented during the summer by companies that either travel, or are based in one place. Usually they are of a repertory type.

Sympathetic Relating to the feelings of a character, and feeling the same emotions for character enhancement.

Take Space To move into a position where there are no obstructions to movement.

Technique A particular practice or exercise that is helpful in some way to creating a total character.

Tempo The variation of rate at which a play is progressing as a whole during the performance.

Tension The controlled flow of energy within the body ready to be used for positive action.

Timbre The quality of the voice that makes it unique and different.

Timing The rate at which lines are said and the time between lines.

Top To make the voice heard above and beyond whatever is already happening on stage.

Tragedy A play of conflict in which the protagonist usually has a flaw that must be overcome or that will overcome him or her.

Upstage The area of the stage farthest from the audience.

Victorian and Edwardian Drama dealing basically with good and evil. This period was also dominated by the melodrama.

Volume The loud and soft range of the voice.

BIBLIOGRAPHY

Albright, Hardie. *Acting: The Creative Process.*
2nd ed. 1974. Dickenson.

Albright, Harry D. *Working up a Part.* 2nd ed.
1959. Houghton Mifflin Co.

Allensworth, Carl, et al. *The Complete Play
Production Handbook.* 1973. T.Y. Crowell.

Aubignac, Francois H. *The Whole Art of the
Stage.* Arno.

Aye, John. *Humour in the Theatre.* 1975. Repr.
Richard West.

Babcock, Dennis & Boyd, Preston. *Careers in
the Theatre.* (Early Career Books Ser.).
1975. Lerner Publications.

Baker, George P. *Dramatic Technique.*
(Theatre, Film & the Performing Arts
Ser.). 1976. Da Capo Press Inc.

Barker, Clive. *Theatre Games.* 1978. Drama
Book Specialists Publishers.

Benedetti, Robert L. *Actor at Work.* rev. & enl
ed. 1976. Prentice-Hall, Inc.

Bergman, Gosta M. *The Breakthrough of
Modern Theatre.* 1978. Cornell University
Press.

Birch, Dorothy. *Training for the Stage.* 1952.
Norwood Editions.

Black, Malcolm. *First Reading to First Night: A
Candid View of Stage Directing.* 1975.
University of Washington Press.

Blunt, Jerry. *Composite Art of Acting.* 1966.
Macmillan Publishing Co., Inc.

Boleslavsky, Richard. *Acting: The First Six
Lessons.* Theatre Arts Books.

Bowskill. *Acting An Introduction.* 1977.
Prentice-Hall, Inc.

Bradby, David & McCormick, John. *People's
Theatre.* 1978. Rowman & Littlefield, Inc.,
Div. of Littlefield, Adams & Co.

Braun, Edward. *The Theatre of Meyerhold:
Revolution on the Modern Stage.* 1979.
Drama Book Specialists Pubs.

Breen, Robert S. *Chamber Theatre.* 1978.
Prentice-Hall, Inc.

Brook, Peter. *The Empty Space.* 1978.
Atheneum Pubs.

Cameron, Kenneth M. & Hoffman, Theodore J.
Guide to Theatre Study, 2nd ed. 1974.
Macmillan Publishing Co., Inc.

Coger, Leslie I. & White, Melvin R. *Readers
Theatre Handbook: A Dramatic Approach
to Literature.* rev. ed. 1973. Scott,
Foresman & Co.

Cohen, Lorraine. *Scenes for Young Actors.* 1973.
Avon Books.

Cohen, Robert. *Acting Professionally.* 2nd ed.
Mayfield Publishing Co.

Cohen, Robert. *Acting Professionally: Raw
Facts About Careers in Acting.* 1977.

Corey, Orlin. *Theatre for Children—Kid Stuff
or Theatre?* 1974. Anchorage Press.

Corrigan, Robert W. *The World of the Theatre.*
1979. Scott, Foresman & Co.

Crampton, Esme. *A Handbook of the Theatre.*
1970. Drama Book Specialists Pubs.

Crawford, Jerry L. & Snyder, Joan. *Acting in
Person & in Style.* 1976. Brown, William C.,
Co., Pubs.

Dalrymple, Jean. *From the Last Row.* 1975.
White, James T., Co.

Darlington, William A. *Through the Fourth Wall.* (Essay Index Reprint Ser.). 1922. Arno.

Dezseran, Louis J. *The Student Actor's Handbook: Theatre Games & Exercises.* 1975. Mayfield Publishing Co.

Duerr, Edwin. *Radio & Television Acting Criticism, Theory & Practice.* 1972. Greenwood Press, Inc.

Engel, Lehman. *Getting Started in the Theater.* 1973. Macmillan Publishing Co., Inc.

Franklin, Miriam A. *Rehearsal: The Principles & Practice of Acting for the Stage.* 1972. Prentice-Hall, Inc.

Goldenberg, Harvey J. *Acting: An Actor's Guide on How to Try to Get Started in the Business There's No Business Like.* 1978. Anthelion Press, Inc.

Hartnoll, Phyllis, ed. *The Concise Oxford Companion to the Theatre.* 1972. Oxford University Press.

Hatlen, Theodore W. *Orientation to the Theater.* 2nd ed. 1972. Prentice-Hall, Inc.

Hayman, Ronald. *Theater & Anti-Theater: New Movements Since Beckett.* 1979. Oxford University Press.

Horton, Louise. *Careers in Theatre, Music & Dance.* 1976. Watts Franklin, Inc., Subs. of Grolier, Inc.

Hyland, Wende & Haynes, Roberta. *How to Make It in Hollywood.* 1975. Nelson Hall, Inc.

Joels, Merrill E. *How to Get into Show Business.* rev. ed. (Communication Arts Bks.). Orig. Title: Acting Is a Business. 1969. Hastings House Pubs, Inc.

Johnson, Albert & Johnson, Bertha. *Drama for Junior High, with Selected Scenes.* 1971. Barnes, A.S., & Co., Inc.

Jones, Henry A. *The Theatre of Ideas.* 1975. Repr. of 1914 ed. Richard West.

Klein, Maxine. *Time, Space & Designs for Actors.* 1975. Houghton Mifflin Co.

Kline, Peter & Meadors, Nancy. *Theatre Student Physical Movement for the Theatre.* 1971. Rosen, Richards, Press Inc.

Langley, Stephen. *Theatre Management in America; Principle & Practice: Producing for the Commercial, Stock, Resident, College & Community Theatre.* 1974. Drama Book Specialists, Inc.

Markus, Tom. *The Professional Actor: From Audition to Performance.* 1978. Drama Book Specialists, Inc.

Marowitz, Charles. *The Act of Being: Towards a Theory of Acting.* 1978. Taplinger Publishing Co., Inc.

Matson, Katinka. *The Working Actor: A Guide to the Profession.* (Handbooks Ser.). 1978. Penguin Books Inc.

McGann, Mary. *Enjoying the Arts-Theatre.* 1977. Rosen, Richards, Press Inc.

McGaw, Charles J. *Acting Is Believing.* 3rd ed. 1975. Holt, Rinehart & Winston, Inc.

McGaw, Charles. *Working a Scene: An Actor's Approach.* 1977. Holt, Rinehart & Winston, Inc.

Moore, Dick. *Opportunities in Acting Careers.* rev. ed. 1975. National Textbook Company.

Moore, Sonia. *Stanislavski System: The Professional Training of an Actor.* rev. ed. 1976. Penguin Books, Inc.

Nahas, Rebecca. *Your Acting Career.* 1976. Crown Pubs., Inc.

Nuttall, Kenneth. *Your Book of Acting.* 1972. Transatlantic Arts, Inc.

Ommanney, Katherine A. & Schanker, Harry H. *Stage & the School.* 4th ed. 1971. McGraw-Hill Book Co.

O'Toole, J. *Theatre in Education: New Objectives for Theatre, New Techniques in Education.* 1977. Verry, Lawrence, Inc.

Passoli, Robert. Book on the Open Theatre. 1970. Bobbs-Merrill Co., Inc.

Pate, Michael. *The Film Actor.* 1969. Barnes, A.S. & Co., Inc.

Pickering, Jerry V. *Theatre: A Contemporary Introduction.* 2nd ed. 1978. West Publishing Co.

Pisk, Litz. *The Actor & His Body.* 1976. Theatre Arts Books.

Poggi, Jack. *Theatre in America: The Impact of Economic Forces.* 1968. Cornell University Press.

Rice, Elmer. *The Living Theatre.* 1972. Greenwood Press Inc.

Rizzo, Raymond. *The Total Actor.* 1975. Odyssey Press.

Roose-Evans, James. *Experimental Theater.* 1971. Avon Books.

Schechner, Richard. *Environmental Theater.* 1973. Hawthorn Books, Inc.

Schevill, James. *Breakout: In Search of New Theatrical Environments*. 1972. Swallow Press.

Scholes, Robert & Klaus, Carl H. *Elements of Drama*. (Orig.). 1971. Oxford University Press.

Schreck, Everett M. *Principles & Styles of Acting*. (Speech & Drama). 1970. Addison-Wesley Publishing Co., Inc.

Shurtleff, Michael. *Audition: Everything an Actor Needs to Know to Get the Part*. 1978. Walker & Co.

Siks, Geraldine & Dunnington, Hazel B., eds. *Children's Theatre & Creative Dramatics*. 1967. University of Washington Press.

Summer, et al. *Actor Training*. Three Brown, Richard ed. 1976. Drama Book Specialists Pubs.

Stanislavski, Constantin. *Actor Prepares*. Theatre Arts Books.

Stanislavski, Constantin. *Actor's Handbook*. Hapgood, Elizabeth R., tr. (Orig.). 1963. Theatre Arts.

Stanislavski, Constantin. *Building a Character*. Theatre Arts.

Stanislavski, Constantin. *Stanislavski's Legacy*. rev. ed. Hapgood, Elizabeth R., tr. (Orig.). 1968. Theatre Arts.

Stanislavsky, Konstantin. *Stanislavsky on the Art of the Stage*. 1967. Faber & Faber, Inc.

Stanislavsky, Konstantin. *Stanislavsky on the Art of the Stage*. Magarshack, David, tr. (Illus. Orig.). 1962. Hill & Wang, Inc.

Stratton, Clarence. *Producing in Little Theatres*. 1975. Richard West.

Styan, J.L. *Elements of Drama*. 1960. Cambridge University Press.

Tanner, Fran A. *Basic Drama Projects*. rev. ed. 1977. Clark Publishing Company.

Taylor, Emerson. *Practical Stage Directory for Amateurs*. 1978. Repr. of 1916 ed. Norwood Editions.

Tompkins, Dorothy L. *Handbook for Theatrical Apprentices: A Practical Guide in all Phases of Theatre*. 1962. French, Samuel, Inc.

Turner, Clifford J. *Voice & Speech in the Theatre*. 3rd ed. 1977. Drama Book Specialists Pubs.

Waller, Adrian. *Theatre on a Shoestring*. (Orig.). 1975. Littlefield, Adams, & Co.

White, Edwin & Battye, Marguerite. *Acting & Stage Movement*. 1978. Arco.

Whiting, Frank M. *An Introduction to the Theatre*. 4th ed. 1978. Harper & Row Pubs., Inc.

Wilson, Edwin. *The Theatre Experience*. new ed. 1975. McGraw-Hill Book Co.

Wright, E. *Understanding Today's Theatre*. rev. ed. 1972. Prentice-Hall, Inc.

Young, John W. *Community Theatre: A Manual for Success*. 1971. French, Samuel, Inc.

Young, John W. *Play Direction for the High School Theatre*. 1973. Kennikat Press, Corp.

INDEX

LANGUAGE ARTS BOOKS

Tandem: Language in Action Series
Point/Counterpoint, *Dufour and Strauss*
Action/Interaction, *Dufour and Strauss*

Business Communication
Business Communication Today!,
  Thomas and Fryar
Successful Business Writing, *Sitzmann*
Successful Business Speaking, *Fryar
  and Thomas*
Successful Interviewing, *Sitzmann and
  Garcia*
Successful Problem Solving, *Fryar and
  Thomas*
Working in Groups, *Ratliffe and Stech*
Effective Group Communication,
  Ratliffe and Stech

Reading
Reading by Doing, *Simmons and Palmer*
Literature Alive, *Gamble and Gamble*
Building Real Life English Skills, *Penn
  and Starkey*
Practical Skills in Reading, *Keech and
  Sanford*
Essential Life Skills Series, *Penn and
  Starkey*

Grammar
Grammar Step-By-Step Vol. 1, *Pratt*
Grammar Step-By-Step Vol. 2, *Pratt*

Speech
Getting Started in Public Speaking,
  Prentice and Payne
Listening by Doing, *Galvin*
Person to Person, *Galvin and Book*
Person to Person, Workbook, *Galvin
  and Book*
Speaking by Doing, *Buys, Sills and Beck*
Self-Awareness, *Ratliffe and Herman*
Literature Alive, *Gamble and Gamble*
Contemporary Speech, *Hopkins and
  Whitaker*
Creative Speaking, *Buys et al.*

Journalism
Journalism Today!, *Ferguson and Patten*

Media
Understanding Mass Media, *Schrank*
The Mass Media Workbook, *Hollister*
Media, Messages & Language, *McLuhan,
  Hutchon and McLuhan*
Understanding the Film, *Johnson and
  Bone*
Photography in Focus, *Jacobs and
  Kokrda*
Televising Your Message, *Mitchell and
  Kirkham*

Theatre
Dynamics of Acting, *Snyder and
  Drumstra*
Play Production Today!, *Beck et al.*
Acting and Directing, *Grandstaff*
An Introduction to Theatre and Drama,
  Cassady and Cassady
The Book of Scenes for Acting Practice,
  Cassady

Mythology
Mythology and You, *Rosenberg and
  Baker*
World Mythology: An Anthology of
Great Myths and Epics, *Rosenberg*

Mystery and Science Fiction
The Detective Story, *Schwartz*
You and Science Fiction, *Hollister*

Writing and Composition
Lively Writing, *Schrank*
Snap, Crackle & Write, *Schrank*
An Anthology for Young Writers,
  Meredith
Writing in Action, *Meredith*
Writing by Doing, *Sohn and Enger*
The Art of Composition, *Meredith*
Look, Think & Write!, *Leavitt and Sohn*
The Book of Forms for Everyday Living,
  Rogers

For further information or a current catalog, write:
National Textbook Company
4255 West Touhy Avenue
Lincolnwood, Illinois 60646-1975 U.S.A.